THE WOMEN'S BOOK OF
POSITIVE
QUOTATIONS
2ND EDITION

Compiled and Arranged
by S. F. Deger and Leslie Ann Gibson

Fairview Press
Minneapolis

Published by Fairview Press, 2450 Riverside Avenue, Minneapolis, Minnesota 55454. Fairview Press is a division of Fairview Health Services, a community-focused health system, affiliated with the University of Minnesota, providing a complete range of services, from the prevention of illness and injury to care for the most complex medical conditions. For a free current catalog of Fairview Press titles, please call toll-free 1-800-544-8207. Or visit our Web site at http://www.fairviewpress.org.

Library of Congress Cataloging-in-Publication Data
The women's book of positive quotations / [compiled and arranged by] S.F. Deger and Leslie Ann Gibson. – 2nd ed.
    p. cm.
  ISBN 978-1-57749-238-2 (alk. paper)
  1. Success—Quotations, maxims, etc. 2. Conduct of life—Quotations, maxims, etc. 3. Women—Quotations. I. Deger, S. F. II. Gibson, Leslie Ann, 1956– III. Title: Book of positive quotations.
  PN6084.S78W58 2010
  082'.082—dc22

                                        2010024463

First edition: 2001
Second edition: 2010
Printed in Canada

15 14 13 12 11 10   7 6 5 4 3 2 1

Book design by Ryan Scheife, Mayfly Design (www.mayflydesign.net)

CONTENTS

INTRODUCTION

Early in 2001, I sent my publisher the final revisions of the first edition of *The Women's Book of Positive Quotations*. It was to be my first book—a monumental anthology of quotations by and about women.

First-time authors are a bit like first-time mothers: anxious and uncertain about the future, yet excited for the day their "babies" will enter the world. Advance copies of the book were scheduled to land on my doorstep in mid-September, a few weeks before the official October publication date. But my anticipation and excitement would be shattered a few days before the books arrived—when terrorists flew two planes into the World Trade Center, a third into the Pentagon, and a fourth into a field in rural Pennsylvania, en route to the U.S. capital.

Everything changed that day; the world became a much more uncertain place. Joy and optimism seemed to get put on hold as we all wondered if this was to be the face of the new millennium. I even felt a bit of metaphoric postpartum depression after the "birthing" of the book. If it weren't for the occasional reader writing to tell me what a comfort the book had been to her during that dark period, I may have questioned my own veracity as a writer, as well as the printed word's ability to effect change in troubled times.

But in the years that followed, we all emerged with a new sense of hope. It wasn't the naive, "think positive thoughts and everything will be OK" idealism that was pervasive before the tragedy. Instead, it was more like the seasoned wisdom one gains after having endured a terrible loss. It was during that time that I decided maybe I needed to revisit this book. I enlisted the help of friends, as well as my dear husband, to bring a communal voice to work—rather than the "I can do it!" individualism of the first edition. I also added thirty-two chapter prefaces that paired original essays with the thoughts of the many famous women whose quotations are reproduced here. Collectively, I think we've managed to invoke an even greater sense of sisterhood, grace, and humility—qualities that I believe have been more deeply woven into the fabric of society over the past decade.

There *is* a certain audacity to hope. For those who are struggling with life's uncertainties, as well as for those who have overcome, it's my hope that this edition will be a welcome bedside reader—a daily reminder of how far we have grown as women and as citizens, and the challenging but inspiring work that still lies ahead of each of us.

—LESLIE ANN GIBSON
MINNEAPOLIS, 2010

Chapter 1

SPARKS OF JOY

We all find happiness in big milestones: a birth in the family, a romantic dinner, a weekend outing with our girlfriends. Joy comes easily when we're celebrating a special day with those we love.

But there's a unique joy in discovering happiness in simple, everyday moments. By letting ourselves daydream about the coming weekend, we can escape the anxiety of a too-busy agenda. By stopping to sample some gourmet cheese, we can turn a routine trip to the grocery store into a supermarket adventure. And by taking a new route on the drive home, we can get a fresh look at our neighborhood and remember what we love about our community.

It's natural to feel a sense of accomplishment by checking things off our to-do lists. Errands? Check. Doctor's appointment? Check. Dinner preparations? Check. When our homes are spot-less, our deadlines are met, and our hair looks flawless, we feel on top of the world. But aren't we trading spontaneous joy for our clockwork efficiency? Wouldn't we rather accept some chaos in our lives, in exchange for finding unex-pected sparks of joy?

Although none of us will ever rank "errands" next to "surprise party" on a list of thrilling activities, we can all learn to find happiness in our ordinary moments. ❧

Paradise is exactly like where you are right
now...only much, much better.

—LAURIE ANDERSON

Time is compressed like the fist I close on my knee...I
hold inside it the clues and solutions and the power
for what I must do now.

—MARGARET ATWOOD

The major job was getting people to understand that
they had something within their power that they
could use.

—ELLA BAKER

Each moment in time we have it all, even when we
think we don't.

—MELODY BEATTIE

Success is getting what you want; happiness is
wanting what you get.

—INGRID BERGMAN

To seek after beauty as an end, is a wild goose chase, a will-o'-the-wisp, because it is to misunderstand the very nature of beauty, which is the normal condition of a thing being as it should be.

—ADE BETHUNE

Happiness consists not in having much, but in being content with little.

—LADY MARGUERITE BLESSINGTON

Eden is that old-fashioned house we dwell in every day without suspecting our abode until we drive away.

—EMILY DICKINSON

Here I am, where I ought to be.

—LOUISE ERDRICH

Whatever is—is best.

—ELLA WHEELER WILCOX

Forget the past and live the present hour.

—SARAH KNOWLES BOLTON

Only when your consciousness is totally focused on the moment you are in can you receive whatever gift, lesson, or delight that moment has to offer.

—BARBARA DE ANGELIS

Losing the future is the best thing that ever happened to me.

—MARILYN FRENCH

Looking repeatedly into the past, you do not necessarily become fascinated with your own life, but rather with the phenomenon of memory.

—PATRICIA HAMPL

Life has got to be lived—that's all that there is to it.

—ELEANOR ROOSEVELT

In great moments life seems neither right nor wrong, but something greater: it seems inevitable.

—MARGARET SHERWOOD

The future is made of the same stuff as the present.

—SIMONE WEIL

Hope costs nothing.

—COLETTE

Think of all the beauty that's still left in and around you and be happy!

—ANNE FRANK

Build a little fence of trust
around today;
Fill the space with loving work,
And therein stay.

—MARY FRANCES BUTTS

It is always the simple that produces the marvelous.

—AMELIA BARR

We are new every day.

—IRENE CLAREMONT DE CASTILLEJO

Happiness is something that comes into our lives through doors we don't even remember leaving open.

—ROSE WILDER LANE

Stretch out your hand and take the world's wide gift of Joy and Beauty.

—CORINNE ROOSEVELT ROBINSON

Chapter 2

AN ACCURATE MEASURE

As children, we had supportive adults in our lives who told us we could do anything. Whatever we wanted to be—astronauts, musicians, or doctors—they urged us to dream big, work hard, and never give up. These mentors gave us confidence and helped us develop a hard-work ethic. They showed us that *attitude* can have as much impact as *aptitude*. We developed a positive worldview because of their encouragement.

But those positive voices from our youth can have an ironic and unintended effect in our adult lives. As we mature, we discover that our dreams sometimes collide with reality—and these collisions may weaken our determination.

For example, no matter how much we study and practice, our passion for art may never be matched by our talent. Although we may have strong political convictions, we may lack the time, energy, and resources to get involved in civic life beyond the neighborhood level. Physical or financial limitations may keep us from achieving other childhood dreams.

Sometimes we simply have to accept our limitations. It's not a matter of giving up; it's about measuring our priorities against a realistic yardstick. And if we find joy in the pursuit, then we shouldn't allow our dreams to fade. Instead, we can focus on the journey instead of the destination. ❧

And remember, expect nothing and life will be velvet.

—LISA GARDINER

One cannot collect all the beautiful shells on the beach.

—ANNE MORROW LINDBERGH

Don't try to teach a whole course in one lesson.

—KATHRYN MURRAY

The whole point of getting things done is knowing what to leave undone.

—LADY STELLA READING

What is destructive is impatience, haste, expecting too much too fast.

—MAY SARTON

I think knowing what you cannot do is more important than knowing what you can.

—LUCILLE BALL

You never conquer a mountain. You stand on the summit a few moments; then the wind blows your footprints away.

—ARLENE BLUM

I like trees because they seem more resigned to the way they have to live than other things do.

—WILLA CATHER

Human beings aren't orchids; we must draw something from the soil we grow in.

—SARA JEANNETTE DUNCAN

If you can keep your head when all about are losing theirs, it's just possible you haven't grasped the situation.

—JEAN KERR

Each of us does, in effect, strike a series of deals or compromises between the wants and longings of the inner self, and an outer environment that offers certain possibilities and sets certain limitations.

—MAGGIE SCARF

Don't spend time beating on a wall, hoping to transform it into a door.

—DR. LAURA SCHLESSINGER

Wisdom never kicks at the iron walls it can't bring down.

—OLIVE SCHREINER

It is impossible to control creation.

—EVELYN SCOTT

Acceptance is not submission; it is acknowledgement of the facts of a situation. Then deciding what you're going to do about it.

—KATHLEEN CASEY THEISEN

Most of us have trouble juggling. The woman who says she doesn't is someone whom I admire but have never met.

—Barbara Walters

Let us accept truth, even when it surprises us and alters our views.

—George Sand (Amantine Dupin)

To have ideals is not the same as to have impracticable ideals.

—L. Susan Stebbing

A pint can't hold a quart—if it holds a pint it is doing all that can be expected of it.

—Margaret Deland

Truth has rough flavors if we bite it through.

—George Eliot (Mary Ann Evans)

What had seemed easy in imagination was rather hard in reality.

—L. M. MONTGOMERY

You can't move so fast that you try to change [a situation] faster than people can accept it. That doesn't mean you do nothing, but it means that you do the things that need to be done according to priority.

—ELEANOR ROOSEVELT

I have been very happy, very rich, very beautiful, much adulated, very famous and very unhappy.

—BRIGITTE BARDOT

Chapter 3

NO TO NEGATIVITY

We've banished our negative thoughts. We've focused on building a positive, affirming world-view. Still, a cloud of negativity sometimes rolls into our lives.

How does it happen? Look around. The people in our lives have a powerful influence on our moods. They can make us soar, or they can drag us down.

We all know women who aren't just positive thinkers; they've made a conscious decision to live a positive life. They assume people have good intentions. They validate and affirm those around them. They mold challenge into opportunity. We're drawn to these women because they inspire us.

Then there are women who radiate negativity. They seem to enjoy pointing out other people's faults. They expect the worst, show disdain for new ideas, and constantly complain about their lives.

Although we admire positive people, negativity has its own power. It's like a virus, silently spreading through a group. The mood subtly shifts, and we find it affecting our own attitude. *That waitress could be more attentive. It is miserably cold outside. This project does seem poorly organized.*

We can reduce our exposure to negative people, but it may be impossible to cut them out of our lives. If they live next door, attend our place of worship, or work beside us, we're stuck with them. Confronting them about their negativity is a possibility, but we have to weigh the potential impact on our relationship.

However, we can remind ourselves that their negative thinking is like a compass that points to an unhealthy destination. And it's a compass we don't have to follow. ◙

The optimism of a healthy mind is indefatigable.

—Margery Allingham

Wrinkles should only indicate where smiles have been.

—Ethel Barrymore

Some knowledge and some song and some beauty must be kept for those days before the world again plunges into darkness.

—Marion Zimmer Bradley

Tears are sometimes an inappropriate response to death. When a life has been lived completely honestly, completely successfully, or just completely, the correct response to death's perfect punctuation mark is a smile.

—Julie Burchill

A sneer is like a flame; it may occasionally be curative because it cauterizes, but it leaves a bitter scar.

—Margaret Deland

High above hate I dwell,
O storms! Farewell.

—Louise Imogen Guiney

Hate is like acid. It can damage the vessel in which it is stored as well as destroy the object on which it is poured.

—Ann Landers

Never say anything on the phone that you wouldn't want your mother to hear at your trial.

—Sydney Biddle Barrows

A critic is someone who never actually goes to the battle, yet who afterwards comes out shooting the wounded.

—Tyne Daly

The weak are the most treacherous of us all. They come to the strong and drain them. They are bottomless. They are insatiable. They are always parched and always bitter. They are everyone's concern and like vampires they suck our life's blood.

—BETTE DAVIS

Grumbling is the death of love.

—MARLENE DIETRICH

Play not with paradoxes. That caustic which you handle in order to scorch others may happen to sear your own fingers and make them dead to the quality of things.

—GEORGE ELIOT (MARY ANN EVANS)

Discussing how old you are is the temple of boredom.

—RUTH GORDON

We criticize and separate ourselves from the process. We've got to jump right in there with both feet.

—Dolores Huerta

Wit is the salt of conversation, not the food, and few things in the world are more wearying than a sarcastic attitude towards life.

—Agnes Repplier

You just can't complain about being alive. It's self-indulgent to be unhappy.

—Gena Rowland

If any has a stone to throw
It is not I, ever or now.

—Elinor Wylie

You live with your thoughts—so be careful what they are.

—Eva Arrington

Cease to be a drudge, seek to be an artist.

—MARY MCLEOD BETHUNE

True revolutions…restore more than they destroy.

—LOUISE BOGAN

There are seeds of self-destruction in all of us that will bear only unhappiness if allowed to grow.

—DOROTHEA BRANDE

We have seen too much defeatism, too much pessimism, too much of a negative approach.

—MARGO JONES

This is the way of peace—overcome evil with good, and falsehood with truth, and hatred with love.

—PEACE PILGRIM

The evil of the world is made possible by nothing but the sanction you give it.

—AYN RAND

Chapter 4

GRACE AND GRATITUDE

Is it selfish to feel relief after hearing about other people's difficulties?

A close friend is diagnosed with a serious illness. Although we're deeply worried for her, we silently count the blessings of our own good health.

Or perhaps a fire destroys a home in our community. We feel compassion, but we're also thankful we're safe and that our possessions are intact.

Gratitude often rises from the most challenging times in life. Whether crisis strikes us or someone we know, we cope by appreciating what we have rather than lamenting what we lack. It's not a selfish reaction; it's a natural one.

The gratitude we feel about our own lives helps us express compassion and assist people in need. Aware of our good fortune, we donate money to the family who survived the fire. We accompany our friend to her medical appointments, and listen thoughtfully when she needs to talk about her illness.

It shouldn't take a tragedy for us to take stock of our good fortune. Taking a daily inventory of our blessings can have the same effect as regularly checking the balance in our financial accounts: a new mindfulness that brings peace to our own daily lives, plus strength in knowing that we have emotional and spiritual riches to share with others. ◉

I have come to understand that every day is something to cherish.

—KERRI STRUG

Glee! The great storm is over!

—EMILY DICKINSON

A woman has got to love a bad man once or twice in her life to be thankful for a good one.

—MARJORIE KINNAN RAWLINGS

Keep a grateful journal. Every night, list five things that you are grateful for. What it will begin to do is change your perspective of your day and your life.

—OPRAH WINFREY

Gratitude unlocks the fullness of life. It turns what we have into enough, and more. It turns denial into acceptance, chaos to order, confusion to clarity. It can turn a meal into a feast, a house into a home, a stranger into a friend. Gratitude makes sense of our past, brings peace for today, and creates a vision for tomorrow.

—Melody Beattie

Blessed are those who can give without remembering and take without forgetting.

—Elizabeth Asquith Bibesco

Remember that not to be happy is not to be grateful.

—Elizabeth Carter

Gratitude weighs heavy on us only when we no longer feel it.

—Comtesse Diane

Appreciation is yeast, lifting ordinary to extraordinary.

　　—MARY-ANN PETRO

My gratitude for good writing is unbounded; I'm grateful for it the way I'm grateful for the ocean.

　　—ANNE LAMOTT

When something does not insist on being noticed, when we aren't grabbed by the collar or struck on the skull by a presence or an event, we take for granted the very things that most deserve our gratitude.

　　—CYNTHIA OZICK

Enjoy the successes that you have, and don't be too hard on yourself when you don't do well. Too many times we beat up on ourselves. Just relax and enjoy it.

　　—PATTY SHEEHAN

I take it as a prime cause of the present confusion of society that it is too sickly and too doubtful to use pleasure as a test of value.

—REBECCA WEST

Silent gratitude isn't much use to anyone.

—GLADYS BRONWYN STERN

A cheer, then, for the noblest breast
That fears not danger's post;
And like the lifeboat, proves a friend,
When friends are wanted most.

—ELIZA COOK

The idea of thanking staff should mean giving them something that they would never buy for themselves.

—JAYNE CROOK

A mother's arms are more comforting than anyone else's.

—DIANA, PRINCESS OF WALES

No matter what accomplishments you make, somebody helped you.

—ALTHEA GIBSON

Much misconstruction and bitterness are spared to him who thinks naturally upon what he owes to others, rather than on what he ought to expect from them.

—ELIZABETH DE MEULAN GUIZOT

Parents, however old they and we may grow to be, serve among other things to shield us from a sense of our doom. As long as they are around, we can avoid the fact of our mortality; we can still be innocent children.

—JANE HOWARD

One can never pay in gratitude; one can only pay "in kind" somewhere else in life.

—ANNE MORROW LINDBERGH

Chapter 5

HELPING OTHERS

We strive to be compassionate women, and we want to support the people we love during difficult times. But it's painful to watch a friend who unwittingly contributes to her own difficulties.

Maybe she keeps getting into unhealthy relationships, or always battles the same problems at work. Her life may be disorganized and chaotic, or perhaps it's so structured and rigid that she's missing spontaneous fun. She knows something isn't working in her life, but she can't — or won't — recognize the problem.

Our frustration boils over when she seeks our advice but ignores it. The solutions are obvious to us, but she seems to be wearing a blindfold. She doesn't seem to gain wisdom from her experiences.

We may have to admit that our help isn't the "right" help. Our solution to a friend's unhealthy relationship may be to end it. Others, however, might encourage her to seek counseling. Problems don't come with one-size-fits-all solutions. Our advice might be perfect—for us. But it's not necessarily the right path for someone else.

Sometimes we have to let go and allow a friend to make mistakes—even repeat her mistakes—no matter how much we care about her. If it's too disturbing to witness her unhealthy choices, we may have to create some space in our relationship. And if she treats us less like a friend than purely as a resource to exploit whenever she's in need—maybe it would be best to end our relationship.

Our desire to help others is deeply rooted, but sometimes we have to love them from a distance. ☙

Sympathy is the charm of human life.

— GRACE AGUILAR

I see their souls, and I hold them in my hands, and because I love them they weigh nothing.

— PEARL BAILEY

One's life has value so long as one attributes value to the life of others, by means of love, friendship, indignation, and compassion.

— SIMONE DE BEAUVOIR

I'd like people to think of me as someone who cares about them.

— DIANA, PRINCESS OF WALES

Tenderness is greater proof of love than the most passionate of vows.

— MARLENE DIETRICH

One of the most valuable things we can do to heal one another is listen to each other's stories.

—REBECCA FALLS

Kindness consists in loving people more than they deserve.

—JACQUELINE SCHIFF

It's a rare thing, graciousness. The shape of it can be acquired, but not, I think, the substance.

—GERTRUDE SCHWEITZER

There are times when sympathy is as necessary as the air we breathe.

—ROSE PASTOR STOKES

As a woman I have no country. My country is the whole world.

—VIRGINIA WOOLF

Don't give advice unless you're asked.

—AMY ALCOTT

Listen long enough and the person will generally come up with an adequate solution.

—MARY KAY ASH

Never help a child with a task at which he feels he can succeed.

—MARIA MONTESSORI

We want to create an atmosphere in which creation is possible.

—MARIE RAMBERT

If you can't be a good example, then you'll just have to be a horrible warning.

—CATHERINE AIRD

Children have more need of models than of critics.

—Carolyn Coats

My playground was the theatre. I'd sit and watch my mother pretend for a living. As a young girl, that's pretty seductive.

—Gwyneth Paltrow

We deceive ourselves when we fancy that only weakness needs support. Strength needs it far more.

—Anne-Sophie Swetchine

What you teach your own children is what you really believe in.

—Cathy Warner Weatherford

In helping others, we shall help ourselves, for whatever good we give out completes the circle and comes back to us.

—Flora Edwards

There is nothing to make you like other human beings so much as doing things for them.

—ZORA NEALE HURSTON

Giving opens the way for receiving.

—FLORENCE SCOVEL SHINN

Fill the cup of happiness for others, and there will be enough overflowing to fill yours to the brim.

—ROSE PASTOR STOKES

Nothing liberates our greatness like the desire to help, the desire to serve.

—MARIANNE WILLIAMSON

Chapter 6

THE JOY OF FRIENDSHIP

If a friend begins volunteering at a homeless shelter, we end up learning about the issues surrounding families in poverty. When a friend raves about a new restaurant, we're definitely going to eat there. And if a friend becomes interested in classical music, we might find ourselves sitting next to her at a concert—maybe for the first time.

Friendship fuels our personal growth. Our friends give us a comfortable way to sample new experiences. They open doors to the world.

It's easy to get caught in routines: following the same route during an evening walk, making the same meals, listening to the same music, shopping at the same stores. Our friends coax us out of familiar territory.

When a friend decides to pursue her dream of becoming a painter, we share the journey as she buys supplies, takes classes, and displays her work. Her enthusiasm is inspiring. Her satisfaction is contagious.

Soon we're reflecting on our own dreams. Whether we've always wanted to explore a creative pursuit, travel somewhere fun, or try a new physical activity—our friends give us inspiration and support. They'll read our poetry or listen to stories about our trip while we show them the photos. They validate our desire to grow and explore the world.

We're not going to enjoy all of our friends' hobbies and adventures. We may disagree with our friend's restaurant review. We may not think she's a talented painter or develop an appreciation for her style. It's not about whether we like the same things. The joy in friendship is the exploration and the sharing. ◉

That's the risk you take if you change: that people you've been involved with won't like the new you. But other people who do will come along.

—LISA ALTHER

Friendship has splendors that love knows not. It grows stronger when crossed, whereas obstacles kill love. Friendship resists time, which wearies and severs couples. It has heights unknown to love.

—MARIAMA BÂ

True friends are those who really know you but love you anyway.

—EDNA BUCHANAN

A friend is someone you can be alone with and have nothing to do and not be able to think of anything to say and be comfortable in the silence.

—SHERYL CONDIE

It's the friends you can call up at 4:00 a.m. that matter.

—Marlene Dietrich

Perhaps the most delightful friendships are those in which there is much agreement, much disputation, and yet more personal liking.

—George Eliot (Mary Ann Evans)

The most beautiful discovery true friends make is that they can grow separately without growing apart.

—Elizabeth Foley

Trouble is a sieve through which we sift our acquaintances. Those too big to pass through are our friends.

—Arlene Francis

I have come to esteem history as a component of friendships. In my case at least friendships are not igneous but sedimentary.

—Jane Howard

The growth of true friendship may be a lifelong affair.

—SARAH ORNE JEWETT

Constant use had not worn ragged the fabric of their friendship.

—DOROTHY PARKER

Even where the affections are not strongly moved by any superior excellence, the companions of our childhood always possess a certain power over our minds which hardly any later friend can obtain.

—MARY SHELLEY

There's no friend like someone who has known you since you were five.

—ANNE STEVENSON

Lots of people want to ride with you in the limo, but what you want is someone who will take the bus with you when the limo breaks down.

—OPRAH WINFREY

I have lost friends, some by death…others by sheer inability to cross the street.

—VIRGINIA WOOLF

Pioneers may be picturesque figures, but they are often rather lonely ones.

—NANCY ASTOR

Friends are the thermometer by which we may judge the temperature of our fortunes.

—LADY MARGUERITE BLESSINGTON

And we find at the end of a perfect day,
The soul of a friend we've made.

—CARRIE JACOBS BOND

Love is like the wild-rose briar;
Friendship is like the holly-tree.
The holly is dark when the rose briar blooms,
But which will bloom most constantly?

—EMILY BRONTË

If you want an accounting of your worth, count your friends.

—MERRY BROWNE

The great difference between voyages rests not in ships but in the people you meet on them.

—AMELIA BURR

Only solitary men know the full joys of friendship. Others have their family; but to a solitary and an exile his friends are everything.

—WILLA CATHER

My friends are my estate.

—EMILY DICKINSON

If I don't have friends, then I ain't nothing.

—BILLIE HOLIDAY

Chapter 7

CARING FOR THE SOUL

We nurture our bodies every day, but what about our souls?

We eat, drink, and sleep because our bodies revolt if we don't. Neglecting our bodies over the long term, through lack of exercise or poor nutrition, translates into illness or chronic disease. Quite simply, our physical needs are impossible to ignore.

But the needs of our souls are not always so apparent. It's sometimes tempting to conquer the day without thinking about our spirituality. When obligations pile up, we tend to skip the practices that nurture our inner lives. We know we've neglected our spiritual needs when we have fleeting moments of despair—those moments when nothing's seemingly wrong in our lives, yet we still feel empty inside.

It's important to tend to our souls. For some of us, quiet reflection in nature is rejuvenating. Others feed spirituality through prayer or meditation. Some of us prefer to read religious texts or interact with our faith community.

How we nurture our souls is less important than ensuring we're committed to doing it on a regular basis.

When our spiritual lives are healthy, we feel a sense of harmony and connectedness with the world. Daily challenges don't overwhelm us because we have perspective. We're grounded, calm, and focused on things that truly matter. We can support and help people in our lives because we're working from a position of inner strength.

Spiritual life is like a moving sidewalk. Whether you go with it or spend your whole life running against it, you're still going to be taken along.

—BERNADETTE ROBERTS

Faith is nothing at all tangible....It is simply believing God; and like sight, it is nothing apart from its object. You might as well shut your eyes and look inside, and see whether you have sight, as to look inside to discover whether you have faith.

—HANNAH WHITALL SMITH

Faith and doubt are both needed—not as antagonists but working side by side—to take us around the unknown curve.

—LILLIAN SMITH

Spirituality leaps where science cannot yet follow, because science must always test and measure, and much of reality and human experience is immeasurable.

—STARHAWK

The best thing must be to flee from all to the All.

—TERESA OF ÁVILA

I believe devoutly in the Word. The Word can save all, destroy all, stop the inevitable, and express the inexpressible.

—NINA VORONEL

A red-hot belief in eternal glory is probably the best antidote to human panic that there is.

—PHYLLIS BOTTOME

If I saw the gates of hell open and I stood on the brink of the abyss, I would not despair, I would not lose hope of mercy, because I would trust in You, my God.

—GEMMA GALGANI

Our body is not made of iron. Our strength is not that of stone. Live and hope in the Lord, and let your service be according to reason.

—SAINT CLARE OF ASSISI

Divine love always has met and always will meet every human need.

—MARY BAKER EDDY

For the truly faithful, no miracle is necessary. For those who doubt, no miracle is sufficient.

—NANCY GIBBS

I would rather walk with God in the dark than go alone in the light.

—MARY GARDINER BRAINARD

God tests His real friends more severely than the lukewarm ones.

—KATHRYN HULME

Out of the chill and the shadow,
Into the thrill and the shine;
Out of the dearth and the famine,
Into the fullness divine.

—MARGARET ELIZABETH SANGSTER

Let nothing disturb you, nothing frighten you; all things are passing; God never changes.

—Teresa of Ávila

There are no atheists on turbulent airplanes.

—Erica Jong

I believe in the immortality of the soul because I have within me immortal longings.

—Helen Keller

A human being does not cease to exist at death. It is change, not destruction, which takes place.

—Florence Nightingale

The accidents of life separate us from our dearest friends, but let us not despair. God is like a looking glass in which souls see each other. The more we are united to Him by love, the nearer we are to those who belong to Him.

—Elizabeth Ann Seton

Impermanence is the law of the universe.

—CARLENE HATCHER POLITE

Faith is an excitement and an enthusiasm, a state of intellectual magnificence which we must not squander on our way through life.

—GEORGE SAND (AMANTINE DUPIN)

Jesus makes the bitterest mouthful taste sweet.

—THÉRÈSE OF LISIEUX

My faith has wavered but has saved me.

—HELEN HAYES

As to the aridity you are suffering from, it seems to me our Lord is treating you like someone He considers strong: He wants to test you and see if you love Him as much at times of aridity as when He sends you consolations. I think this is a very great favor for God to show you.

—TERESA OF ÁVILA

Chapter 8

DISCOVERING OUR STRENGTHS

When we were girls, most of us quickly discovered we had a gift. It may have been in academics or athletics, or maybe our charm and social skills won us a lot of friends. In any case, we sharpened and refined those skills as we grew. These skills, in turn, help shaped the adult women we would ultimately become.

Our talents or hobbies may be so entwined with our identities that people come to know us for them. We're singers, knitters, golfers, decorators, or healers. Friends talk about the incredible meals we make, our sense of fashion, or the way we help people solve problems. We are what we *do*.

So maybe it's time to redefine ourselves — by developing *new* strengths.

If we were clumsy teenagers who couldn't handle a ball, now might be the time to join a community softball team. Or maybe we can finally learn to play that musical instrument that used to cause us so much frustration. The years have changed us; we're more confident and open-minded. We're not impatient little girls anymore — we don't have to become frustrated and quit just because we're not a "natural" in an area of study or practice.

Lifestyle blogs and newsstand magazines are full of stories about women who have reinvented themselves. Whether they've made a personal, educational, or career change, the experience enhanced their lives. Why not join them? Just as discovering our strengths was the most exhilarating part of our youth, it can be the most exhilarating part of our adulthood. The payoff is new hobbies, new friendships, and a deeper sense of self. ✿

The deeper interior you have, the more you have in your library.

—JACQUELINE BISSET

Follow your interests, get the best available education and training, set your sights high, be persistent, be flexible, keep your options open, accept help when offered, and be prepared to help others.

—MILDRED SPIEWAK DRESSELHAUS

It's all to do with the training: you can do a lot if you're properly trained.

—QUEEN ELIZABETH II

There is no good reason why we should not develop and change until the last day we live.

—KAREN HORNEY

We can't take any credit for our talents. It's how we use them that counts.

—MADELEINE L'ENGLE

As it turns out, social scientists have established only one fact about single women's mental health: employment improves it.

—Susan Faludi

We should try to bring to any power what we have as women. We will destroy it all if we try to imitate that absolutely unfeeling, driving ambition that we have seen coming at us across the desk.

—Colleen Dewhurst

As simple as it sounds, we all must try to be the best person we can: by making the best choices, by making the most of the talents we've been given.

—Mary Lou Retton

It is the duty of youth to bring its fresh powers to bear on social progress. Each generation of young people should be to the world like a vast reserve force to a tired army. They should lift the world forward. That is what they are for.

—Charlotte P. Gilman

What is most beautiful in virile men is something feminine; what is most beautiful in feminine women is something masculine.

—SUSAN SONTAG

You must love and care for yourself, because that's when the best comes out.

—TINA TURNER

In order to be irreplaceable one must always be different.

—COCO CHANEL

I looked always outside of myself to see what I could make the world give me instead of looking within myself to see what was there.

—BELLE LIVINGSTONE

The trouble with specialists is that they tend to think in grooves.

—ELAINE MORGAN

Why can a man not act himself, be himself, and think for himself? It seems to me that naturalness alone is power; that a borrowed word is weaker than our own weakness, however small we may be.

—MARIA MITCHELL

So prodigal was I of youth,
Forgetting I was young;
I worshipped dead men for their strength,
Forgetting I was strong.

—VITA SACKVILLE-WEST

Saying "yes" to yourself means acknowledging what you have that's good and working on the things that aren't.

—PATRICIA FRIPP

When you affirm your own rightness in the universe, then you co-operate with others easily and automatically as part of your own nature. You, being yourself, help others be themselves.

—JANE ROBERTS

It is not easy to be sure that being yourself is worth the trouble, but [we do know] it is our sacred duty.

—Florida Scott-Maxwell

Why not be oneself? That is the whole secret of a successful appearance. If one is a greyhound, why try to look like a Pekingese?

—Dame Edith Sitwell

Nature never repeats herself, and the possibilities of one human soul will never be found in another.

—Elizabeth Cady Stanton

Style is something peculiar to one person; it expresses one personality and one only; it cannot be shared.

—Freya Stark

If you put a woman in a man's position, she will be more efficient, but no more kind.

—Fay Weldon

Chapter 9

OUR GREATEST CHEERLEADER

All of us need a champion—one who will never leave, never falter, and never allow seeds of self-doubt to germinate. That champion should be our own inner voice.

Believing in ourselves is a skill that needs practice. For some of us, self-assurance is not instinctive. The confidence we built in child-hood was dismantled by the awkwardness of adolescence. And we've been working to strengthen it since then.

Our confidence is fueled by associating with people who affirm our choices. When people compliment us, praise our work, or generally express their approval, our self-esteem grows. We feel good about our lives.

While affirmation feels wonderful, the most important voice of approval is our own. A strong, positive self-image is the foundation for a healthy and productive life. That's not something that can be fed from the outside; it has to be nurtured from within.

We need—and deserve—to praise ourselves every day, but it's an uncomfortable practice until we make it a routine. Many of us were raised to be champions for others. We learned how to nurture the people in our lives, sometimes at the expense of our own needs, but rarely were we taught how to cultivate our self-confidence.

We're also hesitant to cross the line from confidence into arrogance. It's difficult to tell whether arrogant women are attempting to cover insecurities, or if they're truly conceited. In either case, it's not a quality we want to emulate.

When confidence is woven into our core, it's not easily destroyed by outside forces. We become empowered to make choices that are right for us, and we worry less about the impressions of others. We become our own cheerleaders. ❧

Who we are never changes. Who we think we are
does.

—MARY S. ALMANAC

You cannot belong to anyone else, until you belong
to yourself.

—PEARL BAILEY

Love yourself first and everything else falls into line.
You really have to love yourself to get anything done
in this world.

—LUCILLE BALL

A strong, positive self-image is the best possible
preparation for success.

—DR. JOYCE BROTHERS

No matter what age you are, or what your circumstances might be, you are special, and you still have something unique to offer. Your life, because of who you are, has meaning.

—Barbara De Angelis

I've learned to take time for myself and to treat myself with a great deal of love and respect 'cause I like me.…I think I'm kind of cool.

—Whoopi Goldberg

You are all you will ever have for certain.

—June Havoc

I've finally stopped running away from myself. Who else is there better to be?

—Goldie Hawn

I want to be remembered as the person who helped us restore faith in ourselves.

—Wilma Pearl Mankiller

Life is to be lived. If you have to support yourself, you had bloody well better find some way that is going to be interesting, and you don't do that by sitting around wondering about yourself.

—KATHARINE HEPBURN

The worst walls are never the ones you find in your way. The worst walls are the ones you put there— you build yourself. Those are the high ones, the thick ones, the ones with no doors in.

—URSULA K. LE GUIN

To succeed is nothing—it's an accident. But to feel no doubts about oneself is something very different: it is character.

—MARIE LENÉRU

To make the choice for independent survival, the great man's wife has to become convinced of her own intrinsic worth.

—JOANNA T. STEICHEN

Beauty to me is being comfortable in your own skin.

—Gwyneth Paltrow

I am the only real truth I know.

—Jean Rhys

We must be steady enough in ourselves, to be open and to let the winds of life blow through us, to be our breath, our inspiration; to breathe with them, mobile and soft in the limberness of our bodies, in our agility, our ability, as it were, to dance, and yet to stand upright.

—Mary Caroline Richards

No matter how lonely you get or how many birth announcements you receive, the trick is not to get frightened. There's nothing wrong with being alone.

—Wendy Wasserstein

Love your self's self where it lives.

—Anne Sexton

No man is defeated without until he has first been defeated within.

—ELEANOR ROOSEVELT

Self-esteem isn't everything; it's just that there's nothing without it.

—GLORIA STEINEM

Nobody can be exactly like me. Sometimes even I have trouble doing it.

—TALLULAH BANKHEAD

If you are going to think black, think positive about it. Don't think down on it, or think it is something in your way. And this way, when you really do want to stretch out and express how beautiful black is, everybody will hear you.

—LEONTYNE PRICE

Oh, I'm so inadequate. And I love myself!

—MEG RYAN

Chapter 10

A LITTLE RESTRAINT

Resisting impulse purchases. Walking past the appetizers without stopping to nibble. Skipping an evening with friends to finish an important project. Holding back a snide response to a silly statement.

Self-restraint is among the most coveted of characteristics. No wonder—it's also among the most difficult.

We've read all sorts of advice about holding back our impulses, from deep breathing to counting to ten to substituting another healthier behavior. Those strategies may be helpful, but none of them magically translates into self-control.

If we really want to exercise self-restraint, maybe the most sensible solution is to physically avoid whatever tempts us. If we're not standing near the dessert table, we're less inclined to sample any goodies. We'll only spend the cash we took to the mall as long as we leave the credit card at home.

We can't hide from all our temptations, though, nor would we want to. Who'd skip a friend's birthday party simply to avoid the chocolate cake? In those instances, a compromise is the most sensible solution. We could devour two large pieces of cake and then be upset with ourselves afterward for a lack of self-control. Or, we could enjoy a small slice and praise ourselves for practicing moderation.

Sometimes we need to relax our standards for self-control. Discipline can be healthy, of course, but denial makes life feel repressive and too structured. If we continually deny ourselves, we're going to lose control eventually and then overindulge.

Practicing moderation is like developing a compromise with ourselves—and that's the key to self-restraint. ❧

No matter how lovesick a woman is, she shouldn't take the first pill that comes along.

—DR. JOYCE BROTHERS

He that hath no rule over his own spirit is like a city that is broken down and without walls.

—TAYLOR CALDWELL

We have learned that power is a positive force if it is used for positive purposes.

—ELIZABETH DOLE

You must learn to be still in the midst of activity, and to be vibrantly alive in repose.

—INDIRA GANDHI

A woman that's too soft and sweet is like tapioca pudding—fine for them as likes it.

—OSA JOHNSON

A little of what you fancy does you good.

—MARIE LLOYD

Gammy used to say, "Too much scrubbing takes the life right out of things."

—BETTY MACDONALD

Who is apt, on occasion, to assign a multitude of reasons when one will do? This is a sure sign of weakness in argument.

—HARRIET MARTINEAU

The point of good writing is knowing when to stop.

—L. M. MONTGOMERY

Superior people never make long visits.

—MARIANNE MOORE

The longest absence is less perilous to love than the terrible trials of incessant proximity.

—OUIDA

Never eat more than you can lift.

—MISS PIGGY

I know too well the poison and the sting
Of things too sweet.

—ADELAIDE PROCTOR

Would that there were an award for people who come to understand the concept of enough. Good enough. Successful enough. Thin enough. Rich enough. Socially responsible enough. When you have self-respect you have enough.

—GAIL SHEEHY

To wear your heart on your sleeve isn't a very good plan; you should wear it inside, where it functions best.

—MARGARET THATCHER

For fast-acting relief try slowing down.

—LILY TOMLIN

A little kingdom I possess,
Where thoughts and feelings dwell;
And very hard the task I find
Of governing it well.

—LOUISA MAY ALCOTT

Everybody's business is nobody's business, and
nobody's business is my business.

—CLARA BARTON

I listen and give input only if somebody asks.

—BARBARA BUSH

Too often in ironing out trouble someone gets
scorched.

—MARCELENE COX

When you borrow trouble you give your peace of
mind as security.

—MYRTLE REED

Don't be curious of matters that don't concern you;
never speak of them, and don't ask about them.

—TERESA OF ÁVILA

I believe the sign of maturity is accepting deferred
gratification.

—PEGGY CAHN

Self-denial is painful for a moment, but very
agreeable in the end.

—JANE TAYLOR

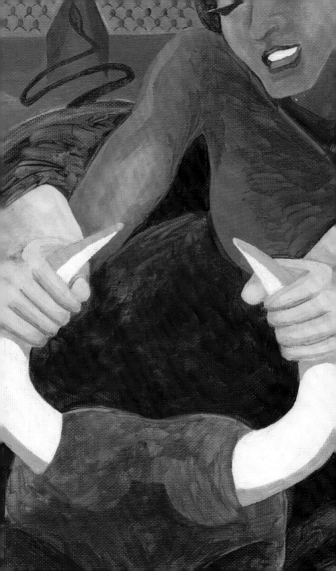

Chapter 11

TAKING CHARGE

Patience is an important skill. So is impatience. Life doesn't come with a rewind button. If we wait to pursue our goals, all we gain is frustration and regret. We need to be rabidly impatient when it comes to things that matter to us. No matter how busy we get, no matter how much other people need us, we deserve to carve out time for ourselves and the activities we want to pursue.

Some days we just get slammed: the refrigerator is leaking, a family member needs an emergency babysitter, and the new puppy chewed up the sofa cushions. All the things we wanted to do—take a walk, finish a project, relax and read the newspaper—take a backseat. Who's in charge here?

Time is the one thing we can't recycle, buy, or sell. We have to use it while we have it.

Sometimes that means making good use of one brief hour even though we wanted an entire day. If we made progress—even if it's small progress—then we should count the time as well spent.

We also have to practice using a key word: "no." Saying no is an essential skill—and an unfortunate necessity. Sometimes we have to use it with the people we care about. We don't want to be selfish, and we don't want to neglect friends and family when they need help. But healthy boundaries help us regain control of our busy lives.

Using our time wisely means more than being efficient. It means we're doing things that are important to us. When it comes to our own lives, we should always be the driver—never the passenger. ❧

With renunciation life begins.

—AMELIA BARR

As I grow older, part of my emotional survival plan must be to actively seek inspiration instead of passively waiting for it to find me.

—BEBE MOORE CAMPBELL

There is only one big thing—desire. And before it, when it is big, all is little.

—WILLA CATHER

Boredom is the fear of self.

—COMTESSE DIANE

It is not opposition but indifference which separates men.

—MARY PARKER FOLLETT

I have always had a dread of becoming a passenger in life.

—MARGRETHE II, QUEEN OF DENMARK

A continued atmosphere of hectic passion is very trying if you haven't got any of your own.

—DOROTHY L. SAYERS

The clue is not to ask in a miserly way—the key is to ask in a grand manner.

—ANN WIGMORE

I don't want to be a passenger in my own life.

—DIANE ACKERMAN

Independence is happiness.

—SUSAN B. ANTHONY

I leave before being left. I decide.

—BRIGITTE BARDOT

Living by proxy is always a precarious expedient.

—SIMONE DE BEAUVOIR

When I saw something that needed doing, I did it.

—NELLIE CASHMAN

No one is in control of your happiness but you; therefore, you have the power to change anything about yourself or your life that you want to change.

—BARBARA DE ANGELIS

Women share with men the need for personal success, even the taste for power, and no longer are we willing to satisfy those needs through the achievements of surrogates, whether husbands, children, or merely role models.

—ELIZABETH DOLE

I never really address myself to any image anybody has of me. That's like fighting with ghosts.

—SALLY FIELD

There is no such thing as vicarious experience.

—MARY PARKER FOLLETT

I love being single. It's almost like being rich.

—SUE GRAFTON

It is better to be tied to any thorny bush than to be with a cross man.

—AUGUSTA GREGORY

I don't follow precedent, I establish it.

—FANNY ELLEN HOLTZMAN

Our concern must be to live while we're alive…to release our inner selves from the spiritual death that comes with living behind a facade designed to conform to external definitions of who and what we are.

—ELISABETH KÜBLER-ROSS

Intimate relationships cannot substitute for a life plan. But to have any meaning or viability at all, a life plan must include intimate relationships.

—HARRIET LERNER

The great law of denial belongs to the powerful forces of life, whether the case be one of coolish baked beans, or an unrequited affection.

—ELIZABETH STUART PHELPS

Who ever walked behind anyone to freedom?

—HAZEL SCOTT

I do not wish women to have power over men; but over themselves.

—MARY SHELLEY

Do not wait for ideal circumstances, nor the best opportunities; they will never come.

—JANET ERSKINE STUART

Chapter 12

WHAT REALLY MATTERS

We've all been victims of the "upsell." Looking for a basic, no-frills refrigerator? Certain sales reps will send us home with the megamodel that does everything except prepare the food inside—and leave us with less money in our purses.

Sometimes we tend to upsell ourselves. Everything we have, and everything we do, could be bigger and better. Our clothes could be trendier. Our living areas could always use redecorating. A new hairstyle might make us look a little more like that model in the advertisement.

Unchecked, that sales voice becomes persistent: *I have designer clothes, but now I want to lose ten pounds and drop a dress size. I've dropped a dress size; now I need new clothes. Preferably new designer clothes.* And so it goes, on and on.

Does any of it really matter? Of course not. We know clothes and home furnishings are just things. We don't feel authentic happiness because of a well-stocked closet. Our happiness stems from our relationships, our health, and the work we do, whether it's raising a family or running an office.

Why, then, is it so easy to let trivial things distract us? Because that sales voice is pervasive and loud. That voice shouts at us from television and radio, from magazines and newspapers, from the Internet and from other people. And sometimes it drowns out our appreciation for simple living.

Today, let's find a little quiet time—away from all that noise—to remind ourselves of what really matters. ❧

Sooner or later we all discover that the important moments in life are not the advertised ones, not the birthdays, the graduations, the weddings, not the great goals achieved. The real milestones are less prepossessing. They come to the door of memory.

—SUSAN B. ANTHONY

If I had one wish for my children, it would be that each of them would reach for goals that have meaning for them as individuals.

—LILLIAN CARTER

Moderation. Small helpings. Sample a little bit of everything. These are the secrets of happiness and good health.

—JULIA CHILD

In violent and chaotic times such as these, our only chance for survival lies in creating our own little islands of sanity and order, in making little havens of our homes.

—SUSAN KAUFMAN

Small kindnesses, small courtesies, small considerations, habitually practiced in our social intercourse, give a greater charm to the character than the display of great talents and accomplishments.

—MARY ANN KELTY

I am beginning to learn that it is the sweet, simple things of life which are the real ones after all.

—LAURA INGALLS WILDER

Age is something that doesn't matter, unless you are a cheese.

—BILLIE BURKE

There are people who have money and people who are rich.

—COCO CHANEL

I want a busy life, a just mind, and a timely death.

—ZORA NEALE HURSTON

I don't think about whether people will remember me or not. I've been an okay person. I've learned a lot. I've taught people a thing or two. That's what's important.

—JULIA CHILD

I'm aiming by the time I'm fifty to stop being an adolescent.

—WENDY COPE

Truth is like heat or light; its vibrations are endless, and are endlessly felt.

—MARGARET DELAND

No one has yet had the courage to memorialize his wealth on his tombstone. A dollar mark would not look well there.

—CORRA MAY HARRIS

Life is about enjoying yourself and having a good time.

—CHER

My mother drew a distinction between achievement and success. She said that achievement is the knowledge that you have studied and worked hard and done the best that is in you. Success is being praised by others. That is nice but not as important or satisfying. Always aim for achievement and forget about success.

—Helen Hayes

The externals are simply so many props; everything we need is within us.

—Etty Hillesum

To me success means effectiveness in the world, that I am able to carry my ideas and values into the world—that I am able to change it in positive ways.

—Maxine Hong Kingston

If I do have some success, I'd like to enjoy it, for heaven's sake! What is the point of having it otherwise?

—Leontyne Price

If you have a good name, if you are right more often than you are wrong, if your children respect you, if your grandchildren are glad to see you, if your friends can count on you and you can count on them in time of trouble, if you can face your God and say "I have done my best," then you are a success.

　　—ANN LANDERS

It is good to have an end to journey toward, but it is the journey that matters in the end.

　　—URSULA K. LE GUIN

I don't want to make money. I just want to be wonderful.

　　—MARILYN MONROE

Money never remains just coins and pieces of paper. Money can be translated into the beauty of living, a support in misfortune, an education, or future security.

　　—SYLVIA PORTER

Chapter 13

ACCEPTING RESPONSIBILITY

When life takes a tough turn, it's tempting to start the blame game. Who caused this mess? The childish voice inside us wants to point fingers. It was him, it was her, it was them.

The bold—and refreshing—thing to do is accept responsibility for the chaos. If there's a problem in our lives, we have to own it.

Accepting responsibility for our problems gives us power. If we had a role in creating the situation, then we have a role in changing it. We have the ability, inner strength, and wisdom to assess the situation and develop solutions. Granted, the solutions might not be easy, but there always are concrete steps we can take to improve our lives.

When we accept responsibility for our problems, it also changes our perspective in our relationships. People who inappropriately try to blame us—and others—for their problems lose their ability to make us feel guilty. If we're in the practice of thinking about personal responsibility, then we have the strength to deflect inappropriate blame and take control of our feelings.

Taking charge of our own lives doesn't mean we'll escape the random nature of life. Accidents happen. We may have the terrible experience of being victimized at some point in our lives. Even if we're clearly not responsible for something that happens, we do have the power to control what happens next.

We're not to blame if someone breaks into our home and steals from us. We can't stop the careless driver who smashes into our parked car. But if we accept responsibility for how we cope with these problems, then we've refused to surrender power over our lives.

Inner strength comes when we embrace responsibility for our actions—and for our reactions. ❧

What we say and what we do ultimately comes back to us so let us own our responsibility, place it in our hands, and carry it with dignity and strength.

—GLORIA ANZALDÚA

It was completely fruitless to quarrel with the world, whereas the quarrel with oneself was occasionally fruitful and always, she had to admit, interesting.

—MAY SARTON

Being black does not stop you. You can sit out in the world and say, "Well, white people kept me back, and I can't do this." Not so. You can have anything you want if you make up your mind and you want it.

—CLARA MCBRIDE HALE

As far as beauty is concerned, in order to be confident we must accept that the way we look and feel is our own responsibility.

—SOPHIA LOREN

What you have become is the price you paid to get what you used to want.

—MIGNON MCLAUGHLIN

In dreams begins responsibility.

—EDNA O'BRIEN

You end up as you deserve. In old age you must put up with the face, the friends, the health, and the children you have earned.

—FAY WELDON

You are the product of your own brainstorm.

—ROSEMARY KONNER STEINBAUM

I long to put the experience of fifty years at once into your young lives, to give you at once the key to that treasure chamber every gem of which has cost me tears and struggles and prayers, but you must work for these inward treasures yourselves.

—HARRIET BEECHER STOWE

Seek not good from without: seek it within yourselves, or you will never find it.

—BERTHA VON SUTTNER

My satisfaction comes from my commitment to advancing a better world.

—FAYE WATTLETON

It is no use blaming the men—we made them what they are—and now it is up to us to try and make ourselves—the makers of men—a little more responsible.

—NANCY ASTOR

Revolution begins with the self, in the self.

—TONI CADE BAMBARA

Nothing strengthens the judgment and quickens the conscience like individual responsibility.

—ELIZABETH CADY STANTON

We make our own criminals, and their crimes are congruent with the national culture we all share. It has been said that a people get the kind of political leadership they deserve. I think they also get the kinds of crime and criminals they themselves bring into being.

—MARGARET MEAD

The way to achieve happiness is to have a high standard for yourself and a medium one for everyone else.

—MARCELENE COX

Every person is responsible for all the good within the scope of his abilities, and for no more, and none can tell whose sphere is the largest.

—GAIL HAMILTON

We are accountable only to ourselves for what happens to us in our lives.

—MILDRED NEWMAN

I attribute my success to this: I never gave or took an excuse.

—FLORENCE NIGHTINGALE

Believe there is a great power silently working all things for good, behave yourself and never mind the rest.

—BEATRIX POTTER

I made the decision. I'm accountable.

—JANET RENO

It's better to light a candle than curse the darkness.

—ELEANOR ROOSEVELT

Lead me not into temptation; I can find the way myself.

—RITA MAE BROWN

We need to restore the full meaning of that old word, duty. It is the other side of rights.

—PEARL S. BUCK

Chapter 14

THE BEST POLICY

A friend tries on an unflattering dress, and we tell her we prefer a different one because of its prettier fabric. We tell our kids that caffeine will stunt their growth, but in truth, we just don't want them developing a taste for expensive caramel mochas.

While honesty is almost always the best policy, we all sometimes engage in this type of innocent deception with those we love. No friend wants to be told she looks fat in a dress—and kids are far more anxious to grow up than they are to forgo sweets. So, now and then, we use little white lies and distracting tricks to steer our loved ones toward better choices.

Wouldn't it be easier just to be brutally honest? Maybe. But "cutting to the chase" can have a cutting effect on people and on our relationships. What good will a direct approach do if we just end up hurting loved ones' feelings — if we lose their trust and respect?

We've all known someone who struggled with this concept: an acquaintance who always said exactly what was on her mind, no matter how rude or hurtful she came across to others. While we may have admired her confidence, we probably kept her at a distance — never fully sharing our joys or concerns — fearing that *we* might be the next victim of her unflinching judgment.

So, in our own lives, we choose to take the more difficult route. We go out of our way to embrace honesty, treat others with respect, and focus on the positive — but we also learn the little social conventions that help us navigate the treacherous waters of delicate feelings. Because in the end, it's gentle love — not brutal honesty — that makes the best policy. ❧

Truth is the vital breath of Beauty; Beauty the outward form of Truth.

—GRACE AGUILAR

Earnestness and sincerity are synonymous.

—CORITA KENT

If one cannot invent a really convincing lie, it is often better to stick to the truth.

—ANGELA THIRKELL

As long as you keep a person down, some part of you has to be down there to hold him down, so it means you cannot soar as you otherwise might.

—MARIAN ANDERSON

Power is the ability to do good things for others.

—BROOKE ASTOR

Character builds slowly, but it can be torn down with incredible swiftness.

—FAITH BALDWIN

Better to be without logic than without feeling.

—CHARLOTTE BRONTË

Be pretty if you can, be witty if you must, but be gracious if it kills you.

—ELSIE DE WOLFE

The whole human race loses by every act of personal vengeance.

—RAE FOLEY

Cruelty is the only sin.

—ELLEN GLASGOW

To be meek, patient, tactful, modest, honorable, brave, is not to be either manly or womanly, it is to be humane.

—JANE HARRISON

Who sows thorns should not go barefoot.

—ITALIAN PROVERB

I never fight, except against difficulties.

—HELEN KELLER

Not observation of a duty but liberty itself is the pledge that assures fidelity.

—ELLEN KEY

A cruel story runs on wheels, and every hand oils the wheels as they run.

—OUIDA

Justice and judgment lie often a world apart.

—EMMELINE PANKHURST

If you give your life as a wholehearted response to love, then love will wholeheartedly respond to you.

—MARIANNE WILLIAMSON

The difference between weakness and wickedness is much less than people suppose; and the consequences are nearly always the same.

—LADY MARGUERITE BLESSINGTON

Our deeds still travel with us from afar, and what we have been makes us what we are.

—GEORGE ELIOT (MARY ANN EVANS)

You must not change one thing, one pebble, one grain of sand, until you know what good and evil will follow on that act.

—URSULA K. LE GUIN

The only causes of regret are laziness, outbursts of temper, hurting others, prejudice, jealousy, and envy.

—GERMAINE GREER

Remember, no effort that we make to attain something beautiful is ever lost.

—HELEN KELLER

Chapter 15

CHANGING PERSPECTIVE

Regret hangs around us like a fog, making it difficult to focus on our future or see our past with clarity.

When we replace regret with perspective, we see that everything we've done, good and bad, has made us who we are today. Regret is a weight that holds us back and prevents us from accomplishing goals. But perspective is a gift. Perspective gives us the insight we need to improve our lives.

Molding regret into perspective isn't easy. When we're in a dark place, it's hard to see our mistakes as fuel for wisdom. We're struggling with guilt, angry at ourselves for making the wrong choice, and afraid we might fail again.

If our decision to move to a new community doesn't work out, we might be overwhelmed with regret. So we move yet again, but this time we find the perfect home: The location is convenient, and the neighbors are wonderful. Perspective tells us one poor choice was an accidental detour to a better place.

Mistakes are evidence that we're leading interesting and fulfilling lives. If we never took any risks, we'd rarely make a mistake. That's a recipe for a dull life, one with shallow relationships, boring activities, and unrealized dreams. Risk is how we discover the world and evolve as women.

As long as we make amends and don't repeat our mistakes, we deserve to free ourselves from the weight of regret. Clinging to the past makes it impossible to build the lives we want to lead. Instead of obsessing about what we should have done, we need to focus on what's important—a future full of opportunity. ❧

Learn to laugh at your troubles and you'll never run out of things to laugh at.

—LYN KAROL

We cannot alter facts, but we can alter our ways of looking at them.

—PHYLLIS BOTTOME

Work is either fun or drudgery. It depends on your attitude. I like fun.

—COLLEEN C. BARRETT

Life is raw material. We are artisans. We can sculpt our existence into something beautiful, or debase it into ugliness. It's in our hands.

—CATHY BETTER

Proust has pointed out that the predisposition to love creates its own objects: is that not also true of fear?

—ELIZABETH BOWEN

It has never been, and never will be easy work! But the road that is built in hope is more pleasant to the traveler than the road built in despair, even though they both lead to the same destination.

—MARION ZIMMER BRADLEY

I invented my life by taking for granted that everything I did not like would have an opposite, which I would like.

—COCO CHANEL

Being tall is an advantage, especially in business. People will always remember you. And if you're in a crowd, you'll always have some clean air to breathe.

—JULIA CHILD

I actually remember feeling delight, at two o'clock in the morning, when the baby woke for his feed, because I so longed to have another look at him.

—MARGARET DRABBLE

Sometimes I found that in my happy moments I could not believe that I had ever been miserable.

—JOANNA FIELD

Teenagers travel in droves, packs, swarms…To the librarian, they're a gaggle of geese. To the cook, they're a scourge of locusts. To department stores, they're a big beautiful exaltation of larks…all lovely and loose and jingly.

—BERNICE FITZ-GIBBON

I keep my ideals, because in spite of everything I still believe that people are really good at heart.

—ANNE FRANK

I do think that being the second [female U.S. Supreme Court justice] is wonderful, because it is a sign that being a woman in a place of importance is no longer extraordinary.

—RUTH BADER GINSBURG

Women forget all the things they don't want to remember, and remember everything they don't want to forget.

—Zora Neale Hurston

Be of good cheer. Do not think of today's failures, but of the success that may come tomorrow.

—Helen Keller

This is the art of courage: to see things as they are and still believe that the victory lies not with those who avoid the bad, but those who taste, in living awareness, every drop of the good.

—Victoria Lincoln

When you're in love, you put up with things that, when you're out of love you cite.

—Judith Martin (Miss Manners)

Happiness is the ability to recognize it.

—Carolyn Wells

I think there is a choice possible to us at any moment, as long as we live. But there is no sacrifice. There is a choice, and the rest falls away. Second choice does not exist. Beware of those who talk about sacrifice.

—MURIEL RUKEYSER

Life has, indeed, many ills, but the mind that views every object in its most cheering aspect, and every doubtful dispensation as replete with latent good, bears within itself a powerful and perpetual antidote.

—LYDIA H. SIGOURNEY

I expect some new phases of life this summer, and shall try to get the honey from each moment.

—LUCY STONE

Love is much nicer to be in than an automobile accident, a tight girdle, a higher tax bracket, or a holding pattern over Philadelphia.

—JUDITH VIORST

Chapter 16

BECOMING AMELIA EARHART

Some people are happy to live passively, but we want to *live*—enthusiastically, creatively, and abundantly.

The difference between merely existing and living is the adventures we undertake. Shaking up our routines and taking chances feed our spirit. Risk doesn't necessarily mean flying around the world like some modern-day Amelia Earhart. Taking a class, joining a club, launching a new business—anything that's new, anything that makes us hesitate for a moment, is a risk.

For some women, risk-taking behavior comes naturally. These women aren't the type to make lists of pros and cons to weigh a big decision— they just plunge. A chance to volunteer for a month in another country? They're packing for the trip before most of us have started weighing the decision.

Sometimes the payoff is a month of misery and loneliness in another country. But more often than not, the outcome is a joyful transformation. They made new friends, learned about another culture, and contributed to the lives of others.

We deserve to live our own adventures. An outgoing woman might need the thrill of organizing a large, important event to get that rush of adrenaline. A more private person might feel her blood pressure rise from the prospect of inviting a few neighbors over for coffee.

Taking risks doesn't mean we'll do so carelessly— even the skydiving thrill seekers make sure their parachutes are in working order. Regardless of where we land on the adventure scale, leaving our comfort zone is the key to an exciting life. ❧

Anything I've ever done that ultimately was
worthwhile...initially scared me to death.

—BETTY BENDER

Attempt the impossible in order to improve your
work.

—BETTE DAVIS

When you make a commitment to a relationship,
you invest your attention and energy in it more
profoundly because you now experience ownership
of that relationship.

—BARBARA DE ANGELIS

Security is not the meaning of my life. Great
opportunities are worth the risks.

—SHIRLEY HUFSTEDLER

It is better to die on your feet than to live on your
knees!

—DOLORES IBÁRRURI

Security is mostly superstition. It does not exist in nature.

—Helen Keller

Only in growth, reform, and change, paradoxically enough, is true security to be found.

—Anne Morrow Lindbergh

Competition can damage self-esteem, create anxiety, and lead to cheating and hurt feelings. But so can romantic love.

—Mariah Burton Nelson

I am willing to put myself through anything; temporary pain or discomfort means nothing to me as long as I can see that the experience will take me to a new level. I am interested in the unknown, and the only path to the unknown is through breaking barriers, an often painful process.

—Diana Nyad

Love, like a chicken salad or restaurant hash, must be taken with blind faith or it loses its flavor.

—HELEN ROWLAND

Providence has hidden a charm in difficult undertakings, which is appreciated only by those who dare to grapple with them.

—ANNE-SOPHIE SWETCHINE

Life is a risk.

—DIANE VON FURSTENBERG

Most people live and die with their music still unplayed. They never dare to try.

—MARY KAY ASH

It is a very dangerous thing to have an idea that you will not practice.

—PHYLLIS BOTTOME

If you risk nothing, then you risk everything.

—GEENA DAVIS

To know that one has never really tried—that is the only death.

—MARIE DRESSLER

If you play it safe in life, you've decided that you don't want to grow anymore.

—SHIRLEY HUFSTEDLER

And the trouble is, if you don't risk anything, you risk even more.

—ERICA JONG

The fearful are caught as often as the bold.

—HELEN KELLER

Inaction, contrary to its reputation for being a refuge, is neither safe nor comfortable.

—MADELEINE KUNIN

We have to keep trying things we're not sure we can pull off. If we just do the things we know we can do…you don't grow as much. You gotta take those chances on making those big mistakes.

—CYBILL SHEPHERD

In the past, few women have tried and even fewer have succeeded.

—ROSALYN YALOW

Chapter 17

DETOURS ON THE JOURNEY

There are times when we can get lost on the road of life, even when we're following our own directions.

And the reason is a mystery. We've followed all the practical tips. We created a life itinerary, broke the journey into smaller steps, mapped out our activities, and made a point of constantly visualizing our final destination. So what happened?

Setting goals is a practical and powerful way to achieve our dreams, but sometimes we need to look back to regain our focus. When we're fixated on our goals, we don't lose sight of *where* we want to go. But sometimes we forget *why* we wanted to go there in the first place.

Maybe we need to reassess and make sure our goals still excite us. We change over time. Our relationships mature, our families' needs change, and the way we think about work and play evolves. If we reassess our goals and decide they're just as important as ever, we'll feel confident we're still on the correct path.

A renewed commitment helps remind us of what we already know—that worthwhile goals require sustained effort. It's easy to stay focused for a while. The difficulty is related directly to persistence.

Looking back also shows us how far we've come. When we acknowledge our progress—and take time to celebrate it—we'll find it easier to regain our focus. Validation is energizing. It helps us find the inner strength to overcome the obstacles of distraction and fatigue.

With time and reflection, we'll discover we were heading in the right direction all along, our destination beckoning to us like city lights on the horizon. ❧

A schedule defends from chaos and whim. It is a net for catching days. It is a scaffolding on which a worker can stand and labor with both hands at sections of time.

—ANNIE DILLARD

You decide what it is you want to accomplish and then you lay out your plans to get there, and then you just do it. It's pretty straightforward.

—NANCY DITZ

When you stop talking, you've lost your customer.

—ESTÉE LAUDER

What does so-called success or failure matter if only you have succeeded in doing the thing you set out to do. The doing is all that really counts.

—EVA LE GALLIENNE

Goals are dreams with deadlines.

—DIANA SCHARF HUNT

Get out of the blocks, run your race, stay relaxed. If you run your race, you'll win. Channel your energy. Focus.

—CAROL LEWIS

Know what you want to do—then do it. Make straight for your goal and go undefeated in spirit to the end.

—ERNESTINE SCHUMANN-HEINK

A good goal is like a strenuous exercise—it makes you stretch.

—MARY KAY ASH

Manual labor to my father was not only good and decent for its own sake, but as he was given to saying, it straightened out one's thoughts.

—MARY ELLEN CHASE

If ambition doesn't hurt you, you haven't got it.

—KATHLEEN NORRIS

It's weak and despicable to go on wanting things and not trying to get them.

—JOANNA FIELD

I have always been driven by some distant music—a battle hymn no doubt—for I have been at war from the beginning. I've never looked back before. I've never had the time and it has always seemed so dangerous.

—BETTE DAVIS

It is good to have an end to journey toward, but it is the journey that matters in the end.

—URSULA K. LE GUIN

Growth is not concerned with itself.

—MERIDEL LE SUEUR

The self-confidence one builds from achieving difficult things and accomplishing goals is the most beautiful thing of all.

—MADONNA

Life is denied by lack of attention, whether it be to cleaning windows or trying to write a masterpiece.

—NADIA BOULANGER

Grudge no expense—yield to no opposition—forget fatigue—till, by the strength of prayer and sacrifice, the spirit of love shall have overcome.

—MARIA WESTON CHAPMAN

To look back is to relax one's vigil.

—BETTE DAVIS

Until I die, I'm going to keep doing. My people need me. They need somebody that's not taking from them and is giving them something.

—CLARA MCBRIDE HALE

If you don't wake up with something in your stomach every day that makes you think, "I want to make this movie," it'll never get made.

—SHERRY LANSING

To tend, unfailingly, unflinchingly, towards a goal, is the secret of success.

—ANNA PAVLOVA

Reappraise the past, reevaluate where we've been, clarify where we are, and predict or anticipate where we are headed.

—TONI CADE BAMBARA

It helped me in the air to keep my small mind contained in earthly human limits, not lost in vertiginous space and elements unknown.

—DIANA COOPER

What allows us, as human beings, to psychologically survive life on earth, with all of its pain, drama, and challenges, is a sense of purpose and meaning.

—BARBARA DE ANGELIS

Chapter 18

TRUSTING OURSELVES

Every now and then, logic and emotion collide. How can something completely sensible make us feel uncomfortable? Why are we compelled to pursue a passion when common sense would suggest it's not right for us?

Our instincts aren't magical forces—they are subtle reminders of prior experiences and the information we've absorbed throughout the years. What's unique about intuition is how quickly it synthesizes all that complex experience and information into a "gut feeling."

It's smart to step back and analyze those feelings: Do they stem from fear? From misinformation or inexperience? If so, we can reassess the situation. The important thing is that we don't ignore our feelings or debate them away.

An odd sense of having met before may lead us into a romance with someone we normally wouldn't consider our "type." Our ethics may tell us we should lend a hand to an acquaintance, but deep inside we may suspect our generosity is being exploited. And though our faith tells us to treat each person as our brother or sister, instinct naturally leads us to hold certain strangers at arm's length.

No matter how much we may *want* to connect with a person, we can't let logic overrule our deepest feelings. We connect with people—or fail to—on levels that can't be explained. Our bodies have a visceral response.

Knowing when to act on that response comes from a learned ability to trust ourselves. When we listen to our inner voice, we'll make the right choices. Sometimes we may defy perceived logic. Our friends and family might want to guide us in a different direction. But in areas of the heart, of creativity, and of how we want to live, denying our instincts in favor of somebody else's logic is to live someone else's life, rather than our own. ❧

I feel there are two people inside of me—me and my intuition. If I go against her, she'll screw me every time, and if I follow her, we get along quite nicely.

—Kim Basinger

You must train your intuition—you must trust the small voice inside you which tells you exactly what to say, what to decide.

—Ingrid Bergman

Every advance in social progress removes us more and more from the guidance of instinct, obliging us to depend upon reason for the assurance that our habits are really agreeable to the laws of health.

—Emily Blackwell

Trust your hunches....Hunches are usually based on facts filed away just below the conscious level. Warning! Do not confuse your hunches with wishful thinking. This is the road to disaster.

—Dr. Joyce Brothers

Every human being has, like Socrates, an attendant spirit; and wise are they who obey its signals. If it does not always tell us what to do, it always cautions us what not to do.

—LYDIA MARIA CHILD

We need to let our intuition guide us, and then be willing to follow that guidance directly and fearlessly.

—SHAKTI GAWAIN

I move on feeling and have learned to distrust those who don't.

—NIKKI GIOVANNI

Instinct is the nose of the mind.

—MADAME DE GIRARDIN

Advice is what we ask for when we already know the answer but wish we didn't.

—ERICA JONG

Doubt yourself and you doubt everything you see. Judge yourself and you see judges everywhere. But if you listen to the sound of your own voice, you can rise above doubt and judgment. And you can see forever.

—NANCY KERRIGAN

I give myself, sometimes, admirable advice, but I am incapable of taking it.

—LADY MARY WORTLEY MONTAGU

I'm often wrong, but never in doubt.

—IVY BAKER PRIEST

Instinct is a powerful form of natural energy, perhaps comparable in humans to electricity or even atomic energy in the mechanical world.

—MARGARET A. RIBBLE

Trusting our intuition often saves us from disaster.

—Anne Wilson Schaef

I go by instinct....I don't worry about experience.

—Barbra Streisand

To Death I yield, but not to Doubt, who slays before!

—Edith M. Thomas

Trust your gut.

—Barbara Walters

Follow your instincts. That's where true wisdom manifests itself.

—Oprah Winfrey

The essential conditions of everything you do must be choice, love, passion.

—NADIA BOULANGER

There is only one history of any importance, and it is the history of what you once believed in, and the history of what you came to believe in.

—KAY BOYLE

Chapter 19

RESPECTING OTHERS

There's a judge in all of us, and she arrives at verdicts quickly. *They spend money recklessly instead of saving for things that matter. She'll never have a genuine relationship if she doesn't learn how to trust people. He's too negative about new ideas to succeed in his job.*

We know it's unhealthy and unproductive to wield the gavel, but sometimes we feel so strongly that it's difficult to be passive observers. When it comes to people we care about, it's nearly impossible to withhold opinions and advice even though it's clear our guidance isn't wanted.

If a close friend seems to be burning through her bank account with a destructive shopping habit, we can't fix her problem, especially if she doesn't believe it's a problem. We can tell her we're no longer comfortable shopping with her.

We can tell her we won't accept gifts she's purchased for us.

However, we can't force a budget on someone who doesn't want one. We might be able to warn her and motivate through fear, but that's not a positive or respectful way to create change in people's lives.

At those moments, it helps to accept ownership of *our* concern—because it truly is our concern—and remember that respect is the foundation of healthy relationships. We show respect by replacing our judgment with tolerance. In return, our tolerance earns us respect.

We don't have to like all the choices our friends make, but healthy relationships make room for differences. Chances are, our friends worry about our own choices from time to time. They could sit in judgment, but what we want and deserve is respect for our decisions—not a ruling on them. ⊘

It is impossible to fulfill the law concerning love for
Me, God eternal, apart from the law concerning love
for your neighbors.

—Saint Catherine of Siena

Service is the rent we pay for the privilege of living on
this earth.

—Shirley Chisholm

Reform is born of need, not pity.

—Rebecca Harding Davis

Nobody who is somebody looks down on anybody.

—Margaret Deland

I am convinced that any feeling of exaltation because
we have people under us should be conquered, for I
am sure that if we enjoy being over people, there will
be something in our manner which will make them
dislike being under us.

—Mary Parker Follett

"Honesty" without compassion and understanding is not honesty, but subtle hostility.

—ROSE N. FRANZBLAU

It's compassion that makes gods of us.

—DOROTHY GILMAN

The sexes in each species of beings…are always true equivalents—equals but not identicals.

—ANTOINETTE BROWN BLACKWELL

The best index to a person's character is (a) how he treats people who can't do him any good, and (b) how he treats people who can't fight back.

—ABIGAIL VAN BUREN

Theories and goals of education don't matter a whit if you do not consider your students to be human beings.

—LOU ANN WALKER

I believe every person has the ability to achieve something important, and with that in mind I regard everyone as special.

—MARY KAY ASH

The fact that we are human beings is infinitely more important than all the peculiarities that distinguish human beings from one another.

—SIMONE DE BEAUVOIR

To understand another human being you must gain some insight into the conditions which made him what he is.

—MARGARET BOURKE-WHITE

The deadliest feeling that can be offered to a woman is pity.

—VICKI BAUM

Religion without humanity is a poor human stuff.

—SOJOURNER TRUTH

Like snowflakes, the human pattern is never cast twice. We are uncommonly and marvelously intricate in thought and action.

—ALICE CHILDRESS

Everyone needs to be valued. Everyone has the potential to give something back.

—DIANA, PRINCESS OF WALES

Every human being is trying to say something to others. Trying to cry out I am alive, notice me! Speak to me! Confirm that I am important, that I matter!

—MARION D. HANKS

Tyranny and anarchy are alike incompatible with freedom, security, and the enjoyment of opportunity.

—JEANE KIRKPATRICK

Because you're not what I would have you be, I blind myself to who, in truth, you are.

—MADELEINE L'ENGLE

We cannot safely assume that other people's minds work on the same principles as our own. All too often, others with whom we come in contact do not reason as we reason, or do not value the things we value, or are not interested in what interests us.

—ISABEL BRIGGS MYERS

To have one's individuality completely ignored is like being pushed quite out of life. Like being blown out as one blows out a light.

—EVELYN SCOTT

It's funny how your initial approach to a person can determine your feelings toward them, no matter what facts develop later on.

—DOROTHY UHNAK

Nobody really knows Indians who cheat them and treat them badly.

—SARAH WINNEMUCCA

Chapter 20

WORKING TOGETHER

Consider the challenge of starting a new exercise routine—waking up early, getting ourselves to the gym, pushing our bodies to the point of exhaustion. And doing it over and over. Before we know it, we're hitting the snooze button and skipping the gym. We push aside our discouragement and promise ourselves we'll get back on track tomorrow. But it's a promise we struggle to keep.

Now insert a best friend into the scenario. It's difficult to skip a workout when she is expecting us, and it's easier to persist when there's an external voice encouraging us. The mutual support gives us the energy and tools to overcome obstacles. When we hit milestones, we celebrate them together.

Teamwork doesn't mean we should give up on independence or think that we can't do things ourselves. Working together is simply a way to lighten the load and, hopefully, the mood. We can inject a little laughter into a tedious activity when we team up with another person.

Sometimes teamwork is less efficient than working alone. When we're facing a project deadline, we work faster if we can close the door and roll up our sleeves. We don't have to sort through competing ideas and opinions; we don't have to negotiate problems or develop compromises.

But those varied ideas and opinions turn a good project into a great project. Our collective wisdom and experience generate a better outcome. The solo effort might be more efficient, but perhaps it's less effective.

Conquering a challenge by ourselves brings an undeniable surge of pride, but some challenges are made for two—or more. ◈

If enough people think of a thing and work hard enough at it, I guess it's pretty nearly bound to happen, wind and weather permitting.

—LAURA INGALLS WILDER

We learn best to listen to our own voices if we are listening at the same time to other women—whose stories, for all our differences, turn out, if we listen well, to be our stories also.

—BARBARA DEMING

Competition is about passion for perfection, and passion for other people who join in this impossible quest.

—MARIAH BURTON NELSON

Happiness is a sunbeam which may pass through a thousand bosoms without losing a particle of its original ray; nay, when it strikes on a kindred heart, like the converged light on a mirror, it reflects itself with redoubled brightness. It is not perfected till it is shared.

—JANE PORTER

The tourist may complain of other tourists, but he would be lost without them.

—AGNES REPPLIER

Most leaders are indispensable, but to produce a major social change, many ordinary people must also be involved.

—ANNE FIROR SCOTT

You've got to be willing to stay committed to someone over the long run, and sometimes it doesn't work out. But often if you become real honest with yourself and honest with each other, and put aside whatever personal hurt and disappointment you have to really understand yourself and your spouse, it can be the most wonderful experience you've ever had.

—HILLARY RODHAM CLINTON

We must stand together; if we don't, there will be no victory for any one of us.

—MOTHER JONES

I've always believed that one woman's success can only help another woman's success.

—GLORIA VANDERBILT

Alone we can do so little; together we can do so much.

—HELEN KELLER

We all act as hinges—fortuitous links between other people.

—PENELOPE LIVELY

We seldom stop to think how many people's lives are entwined with our own. It is a form of selfishness to imagine that every individual can operate on his own or can pull out of the general stream and not be missed.

—IVY BAKER PRIEST

There's a thread that binds all of us together, pull one end of the thread, the strain is felt all down the line.

—ROSAMOND MARSHALL

My whole life, whether it be long or short, shall be devoted to your service and the service of our great imperial family to which we all belong. But I shall not have the strength to carry out this resolution alone unless you join in it with me.

—Queen Elizabeth II

A person who believes…that there is a whole of which one is a part, and that in being a part one is whole: such a person has no desire whatever, at any time, to play God. Only those who have denied their being yearn to play at it.

—Ursula K. Le Guin

Unless I am a part of everything I am nothing.

—Penelope Lively

For what is done or learned by one class of women becomes, by virtue of their common womanhood, the property of all women.

—Elizabeth Blackwell

Today whenever women gather together it is not necessarily nurturing. It is coalition building. And if you feel the strain, you may be doing some good work.

—BERNICE JOHNSON REAGON

Women's art, though created in solitude, wells up out of community. There is, clearly, both enormous hunger for the work thus being diffused, and an explosion of creative energy, bursting through the coercive choicelessness of the system on whose boundaries we are working.

—ADRIENNE RICH

That is always our problem, not how to get control of people, but how all together we can get control of a situation.

—MARY PARKER FOLLETT

The streams which would otherwise diverge to fertilize a thousand meadows, must be directed into one deep narrow channel before they can turn a mill.

—ANNA JAMESON

Chapter 21

BROADENING OUR HORIZONS

Our worldly perspective tends to shrink when we do the same things day after day, week after week.

But there is a larger world out there, begging to be explored. The great thing is, we don't need a two-week vacation or an airline ticket to see it. A computer with an Internet connection can take us to lands we've never visited. A well-stocked supermarket provides everything we need to experience another culture through an ethnic meal. The nonfiction section of the local library can help us learn about exotic aspects of nature. Whether we're interested in faraway places, the richness of culture, or Earth's biodiversity, we can learn so much about the world right in our own backyard.

And the greatest assets within our communities are the residents whose heritage can enrich our own. Our circle of friends weaves through a wealth of experiences and perspectives. When the circle grows, so do our minds. We can learn about the sights and smells of a land we've never seen by listening to other people's stories. We can understand rituals, cultural practices, and philosophies by interacting with people whose upbringing was different from our own.

New relationships also give us a chance to share our heritage. When we reach out to others, they reach back. We create a little more understanding in the world and make it a bigger—and richer—place for all of us. ❧

I always keep myself in a position of being a student.

—JACKIE JOYNER-KERSEE

When one paints an ideal, one does not need to limit one's imagination.

—ELLEN KEY

Her curiosity instructed her more than the answers she was given.

—CLARICE LISPECTOR

I want, by understanding myself, to understand others. I want to be all that I am capable of becoming.

—KATHERINE MANSFIELD

New things cannot come where there is no room.

—MARLO MORGAN

I think the key is for women not to set any limits.

—MARTINA NAVRATILOVA

I think, at a child's birth, if a mother could ask a fairy godmother to endow it with the most useful gift, that gift should be curiosity.

—ELEANOR ROOSEVELT

On the human chessboard, all moves are possible.

—MIRIAM SCHIFF

I'll always push the envelope. To me, the ultimate sin in life is to be boring. I don't play it safe.

—CYBILL SHEPHERD

Success is not a doorway, it's a staircase.

—DOTTIE WALTERS

Change is the watchword of progression. When we tire of well-worn ways, we seek for new. This restless craving in the souls of men spurs them to climb, and to seek the mountain view.

—ELLA WHEELER WILCOX

The state of the world today demands that women become less modest and dream/plan/act/risk on a larger scale.

—CHARLOTTE BUNCH

I might have been born in a hovel but I am determined to travel with the wind and the stars.

—JACQUELINE COCHRAN

The brain is wider than the sky.

—EMILY DICKINSON

My motto: sans limites.

—ISADORA DUNCAN

If we could only give, just once, the same amount of reflection to what we want to get out of life that we give to the question of what to do with a two weeks' vacation, we would be startled at our false standards and the aimless procession of our busy days.

—DOROTHY CANFIELD FISHER

So long as we think dugout canoes are the only possibility—all that is real or can be real—we will never see the ship, we will never feel the free wind blow.

—Sonia Johnson

Our visions begin with our desires.

—Audre Lorde

A lot of young girls have looked to their career paths and have said they'd like to be chief. There's been a change in the limits people see.

—Wilma Pearl Mankiller

[My father] said, Don't grow up to be a woman, and what he meant by that was, a housewife…without any interests.

—Maria Goeppert Mayer

Man can only receive what he sees himself receiving.

—Florence Scovel Shinn

Our being is subject to all the chances of life. There are so many things we are capable of, that we could be or do. The potentialities are so great that we never, any of us, are more than one-fourth fulfilled.

—KATHERINE ANNE PORTER

Every man is free to rise as far as he's able or willing, but the degree to which he thinks determines the degree to which he'll rise.

—AYN RAND

What else are we gonna live by if not dreams? We need to believe in something. What would really drive us crazy is to believe this reality we run into every day is all there is. If I don't believe that there's a happy ending out there—that will-you-marry-me in the sky—I can't keep working today.

—JILL ROBINSON

Reach high, for stars lie hidden in your soul. Dream deep, for every dream precedes the goal.

—PAMELA VAULL STARR

Chapter 22

INFLUENCING OTHERS

Our teachers and mentors fed our dreams and taught us to persevere. And while their words were influential, we found even greater inspiration from their attitudes, behaviors, and accomplishments.

Now we're the ones in positions of influence. Maybe we have important jobs, or maybe we're role models for the children in our extended families. In either case, we have opportunities to have a positive impact on others through our own actions.

For example, instead of lecturing people about a clean environment, we can demonstrate our point by recycling, working on cleanup projects, and purchasing products that don't degrade the planet. We gain credibility when our words are in sync with our actions.

If we're in a position to exert influence, we also have responsibilities. The people who respect us deserve honesty, reliability, and good judgment. We'll make mistakes, of course, because we're human. No matter how much experience and wisdom we accumulate, we'll eventually do something wrong. But those mistakes don't necessarily threaten our influence. In fact, mistakes can enhance our standing if we acknowledge them gracefully and demonstrate how we learn from them.

It's a privilege to be in a position of influence. We can change people's perspectives, and we can modify their behaviors. But most significantly, by following the examples of our mentors, we can encourage others on their own voyages of self-discovery. ❧

People will support that which they help to create.

—MARY KAY ASH

Those who trust us educate us.

—GEORGE ELIOT (MARY ANN EVANS)

The manager cannot share his power with division superintendent or foreman or workman, but he can give them opportunities for developing their power.

—MARY PARKER FOLLETT

There is nothing better than the encouragement of a good friend.

—KATHERINE HATHAWAY

Nothing fruitful ever comes when plants are forced to flower in the wrong season.

—BETTE BAO LORD

The best direction is the least possible direction.

—JOAN MANLEY

Hold up to him his better self, his real self that can dare and do and win out...People radiate what is in their minds and in their hearts.

—Eleanor H. Porter

Coercion. The unpardonable crime.

—Dorothy Miller Richardson

People who make some other person part of their job are dangerous.

—Dorothy L. Sayers

In my experience, there is only one motivation, and that is desire. No reasons or principle contain it or stand against it.

—Jane Smiley

Diplomacy is the art of letting someone have your way.

—Daniele Vare

Remember, the bread you meet each day is still rising.
Don't scare the dough.

—MACRINA WIEDERKEHR

Praise is the only gift for which people are really
grateful.

—LADY MARGUERITE BLESSINGTON

I praise loudly; I blame softly.

—CATHERINE II

Love makes the wildest spirit tame, and the tamest
spirit wild.

—ALEXIS DELP

There isn't much that tastes better than praise from
those who are wise and capable.

—SELMA LAGERLÖF

What you praise you increase.

—CATHERINE PONDER

What men and women need is encouragement.... Instead of always harping on a man's faults, tell him of his virtues. Try to pull him out of his rut of bad habits.

—Eleanor H. Porter

You take people as far as they will go, not as far as you would like them to go.

—Jeannette Rankin

To hear how special and wonderful we are is endlessly enthralling.

—Gail Sheehy

There is nothing stronger in the world than gentleness.

—Han Suyin

To feel valued, to know, even if only once in a while, that you can do a job well is an absolutely marvelous feeling.

—BARBARA WALTERS

I don't give advice. I can't tell anybody what to do. Instead I say this is what we know about this problem at this time. And here are the consequences of these actions.

—DR. JOYCE BROTHERS

Chapter 23

TAKING ONE DAY AT A TIME

When problems overwhelm us and the pain cuts deep, we can barely manage to breathe, let alone think about recovery. It seems as though no amount of love and support can guide us through.

During these times, all we can do is focus on surviving in the moment. What needs to be done right now? If we can accomplish one small task, then we can think about the next task in line. In between those tasks, we need to grant ourselves time to heal, reflect, and rest.

Pushing through the days, just one at a time, brings us closer to a better place. Over time, we learn to accept loss, deal with failure, and cope with rejection. We move on with our lives. We're not necessarily unscarred, but we do move forward. Time brings us better days.

Doing normal activities won't feel normal, but routines keep us grounded. Simple activities help us survive the day. Just standing in front of the mirror and practicing a smile can make a difference. Even if that smile doesn't feel genuine, it reminds us that we've had smileworthy days in the past, and we'll have more in the future.

The sympathy and support of the people in our lives bring some comfort. When people acknowledge the difficulty of our circumstances, it somehow validates our pain and sustains us. The struggle becomes a little easier.

Years later, we can look back and assess our difficult journey. When we see how far we came, we can credit ourselves for resilience and rebuilding our lives. ❧

The world doesn't come to the clever folks, it comes to the stubborn, obstinate, one-idea-at-a-time people.

—MARY ROBERTS RINEHART

Happiness is a tide: it carries you only a little way at a time; but you have covered a vast space before you know that you are moving at all.

—MARY ADAMS

I never stop to plan. I take things step-by-step.

—MARY MCLEOD BETHUNE

Youth is the time of getting, middle age of improving, and old age of spending.

—ANNE BRADSTREET

You don't just luck into things.... You build step by step, whether it's friendships or opportunities.

—BARBARA BUSH

If we take care of the moments, the years will take care of themselves.

—MARIA EDGEWORTH

My parents told me that people will never know how long it takes you to do something. They will only know how well it is done.

—NANCY HANKS

The only way to find out if you can write is to set aside a certain period every day and try. Save enough money to give yourself six months to be a full-time writer. Work every day and the pages will pile up.

—JUDITH KRANTZ

There are very few human beings who receive the truth, complete and staggering, by instant illumination. Most of them acquire it fragment by fragment, on a small scale, by successive developments, cellularly, like a laborious mosaic.

—ANAÏS NIN

It is not the straining for great things that is most effective; it is the doing the little things, the common duties, a little better and better.

—ELIZABETH STUART PHELPS

Instead of thinking about where you are, think about where you want to be. It takes twenty years of hard work to become an overnight success.

—DIANA RANKIN

One only gets to the top rung of the ladder by steadily climbing up one at a time, and suddenly all sorts of powers, all sorts of abilities which you thought never belonged to you—suddenly become within your own possibility and you think, "Well, I'll have a go, too."

—MARGARET THATCHER

Human successes, like human failures, are composed of one action at a time and achieved by one person at a time.

—PATTY H. SAMPSON

It takes time, love, and support to find peace with the restless one.

—DEIDRE SARAULT

Inspiration does not come like a bolt, nor is it kinetic energy striving, but it comes to us slowly and quietly and all the time.

—BRENDA UELAND

The growth of understanding follows an ascending spiral rather than a straight line.

—JOANNA FIELD

I look at victory as milestones on a very long highway.

—JOAN BENOIT SAMUELSON

It's a long old road, but I know I'm gonna find the end.

—BESSIE SMITH

Home wasn't built in a day.

—JANE ACE

No first step can be really great; it must of necessity possess more of prophecy than of achievement; nevertheless it is by the first step that a man marks the value, not only of his cause, but of himself.

—KATHERINE CECIL THURSTON

Cultural transformation announces itself in sputtering fits and starts, sparked here and there by minor incidents, warmed by new ideas that may smolder for decades. In many different places, at different times, the kindling is laid for the real conflagration—the one that will consume the old landmarks and alter the landscape forever.

—MARILYN FERGUSON

Connections are made slowly, sometimes they grow underground.

—MARGE PIERCY

Chapter 24

MAKING OUR OWN LUCK

A woman who labels herself "unlucky" tends to see life as a random roll of the dice. In her mind, the world's successful people merely managed to beat the odds—effortlessly landing in the right place, at the right time, with the right people. Such a woman may see herself, like others who are less fortunate, as a victim of circumstances beyond her control.

While successful women realize how fortunate they are to know the right people, they also realize that these relationships are no coincidence. More often, they used their social skills and exuberant personalities to build an extensive network, a network they can tap into when they need it.

Successful women do stumble onto opportunity, but it's no fluke. It's because they've planned, sacrificed, and worked hard so they're ready to dive in when opportunity presents itself. They consistently treat luck as work in disguise.

Successful women also can take pride in their accomplishments, and take credit for their success. They know their good fortune isn't an accident. They made it happen through preparation and effort. Nobody can dismiss their accomplishments as the hand of fate.

We empower ourselves when we accept luck as something that's created. If we believe we can turn chance encounters with new people into important connections, then we're going to cultivate relationships. We'll seek opportunity and take risks. We'll never be passive participants in our own lives.

When we believe good fortune is a choice, we'll open ourselves to the world—and luck will follow. ❧

Good luck needs no explanation.

—SHIRLEY TEMPLE BLACK

Most of life is choices, and the rest is pure dumb luck.

—MARIAN ERICKSON

Faith is not belief. Belief is passive. Faith is active.

—EDITH HAMILTON

Every thought we think is creating our future.

—LOUISE L. HAY

Anyone who has gumption knows what it is, and anyone who hasn't can never know what it is.

—L. M. MONTGOMERY

Life is like a mirror. Smile at it and it smiles back at you.

—PEACE PILGRIM

Miracles occur naturally as expressions of love. The real miracle is the love that inspires them. In this sense everything that comes from love is a miracle.

—MARIANNE WILLIAMSON

The doors we open and close each day decide the lives we live.

—FLORA WHITTEMORE

There is no such thing as making the miracle happen spontaneously and on the spot. You've got to work.

—MARTINA ARROYO

I don't know anything about luck. I've never banked on it, and I'm afraid of people who do. Luck to me is something else; hard work and realizing what is opportunity and what isn't.

—LUCILLE BALL

I don't believe in luck. We make our own good fortune.

— DR. JOYCE BROTHERS

Luck is not chance, it's toil: fortune's expensive smile is earned.

— EMILY DICKINSON

You have to learn the rules of the game. And then you have to play better than anyone else.

— DIANNE FEINSTEIN

The one important thing I've learned over the years is the difference between taking one's work seriously and taking one's self seriously. The first is imperative and the second is disastrous.

— MARGOT FONTEYN

The more you invest in a marriage, the more valuable it becomes.

— AMY GRANT

Love doesn't just sit there, like a stone, it has to be made, like bread; remade all the time, made new.

—Ursula K. Le Guin

Some people go through life trying to find out what the world holds for them only to find out too late that it's what they bring to the world that really counts.

—L. M. Montgomery

Pennies do not come from heaven—they have to be earned here on earth.

—Margaret Thatcher

Foolish indeed are those who trust to fortune.

—Lady Murasaki

The worst cynicism: a belief in luck.

—Joyce Carol Oates

I was born lucky, and I have lived lucky. What I had was used. What I still have is being used. Lucky.

—KATHARINE HEPBURN

Don't wait for your "ship to come in," and feel angry and cheated when it doesn't. Get going with something small.

—IRENE KASSORLA

Never grow a wishbone, daughter, where a backbone ought to be.

—CLEMENTINE PADDLEFORD

Don't sit down and wait for the opportunities to come; you have to get up and make them.

—MADAME C. J. WALKER

Chapter 25

WORKING HARD

When we throw ourselves into our work, time seems to pass in a happy blur. At the end of a productive day, we go to bed with a sense of satisfaction, knowing we didn't waste our time.

Extreme mental effort can be as exhausting as physical labor. If we drain ourselves creatively, solve a complex problem, or plow through a stack of paperwork, we're just as tired as the women who painted their homes or ran a marathon.

But the rewards of physical and mental activity are often quite different. We don't win a trophy at the end of the day for having dealt with difficult people. We may have inner satisfaction from working through a tough problem, but we don't get to stand back and marvel at the finished product, whether it's an organized garage, a stack of clean laundry, or a newly planted garden.

We have proof that we gave one hundred percent when our muscles hurt at the end of the day. Fatigue is deeply satisfying when it follows an accomplishment. It's our bodies' way of acknowledging a job well done.

Hard work also is a healthy coping mechanism. Stress builds up in our bodies. We feel tension in our muscles and pressure in our heads. Agitation is released by physical effort—it's like opening a valve that allows stress to seep from our bodies.

The best thing about hard work is its built-in trade-off: When we work hard, it's easier to give ourselves permission to play hard. ❧

I am enjoying to a full that period of reflection which is the happiest conclusion to a life of action.

—WILLA CATHER

If your dream is a big dream, and if you want your life to work on the high level that you say you do, there's no way around doing the work it takes to get you there.

—JOYCE CHAPMAN

Hard work has made it easy. That is my secret. That is why I win.

—NADIA COMANECI

The only thing that separates successful people from the ones who aren't is the willingness to work very, very hard.

—HELEN GURLEY BROWN

It's not the having, it's the getting.

—ELIZABETH TAYLOR

You can have unbelievable intelligence, you can have connections, you can have opportunities fall out of the sky. But in the end, hard work is the true, enduring characteristic of successful people.

—Marsha Evans

Opportunities are usually disguised as hard work, so most people don't recognize them.

—Ann Landers

Winning the [Nobel] prize wasn't half as exciting as doing the work itself.

—Maria Goeppert Mayer

Passion is never enough; neither is skill.

—Toni Morrison

Success depends in a very large measure upon individual initiative and exertion, and cannot be achieved except by a dint of hard work.

—Anna Pavlova

Nobody ever drowned in his own sweat.

—Ann Landers

There are two kinds of talents, man-made talent and God-given talent. With man-made talent you have to work very hard. With God-given talent, you just touch it up once in a while.

—Pearl Bailey

The sport I love has taken me around the world and shown me many things.

—Bonnie Blair

I realized that with hard work, the world was your oyster. You could do anything you wanted to do. I learned that at a young age.

—Chris Evert

It is not hard work that is dreary; it is superficial work.

—Edith Hamilton

When we do the best that we can, we never know what miracle is wrought in our life, or in the life of another.

—Helen Keller

There are no shortcuts to any place worth going.

—Beverly Sills

I like to deliver more than I promise instead of the other way around.

—Dorothy Uhnak

In the spring, at the end of the day, you should smell like dirt.

—Margaret Atwood

If you want something done, ask a busy person to do it. The more things you do, the more you can do.

—Lucille Ball

With the power of conviction, there is no sacrifice.

—PAT BENATAR

I believe you are your work. Don't trade the stuff of your life, time, for nothing more than dollars. That's a rotten bargain.

—RITA MAE BROWN

When you're following your energy and doing what you want all the time, the distinction between work and play dissolves.

—SHAKTI GAWAIN

Work is the thing that stays. Work is the thing that sees us through.

—ELLEN GILCHRIST

Energy is the power that drives every human being. It is not lost by exertion but maintained by it, for it is a faculty of the psyche.

—GERMAINE GREER

Chapter 26

STICKING WITH IT

We have every intention of sticking like glue to our goals. But then life spins out of control. Months—sometimes years—can slip away before we realize we've lost our way. It's discouraging to feel life is passing by, while we're still the same distance from the same dream.

It's never too late to reclaim control and start with a new plan. Instead of viewing a goal as one insurmountable task, maybe we need to divide it into many smaller steps. Regular progress fuels our commitment. The progress might be inches instead of miles, but it's genuine movement nonetheless. And it's certainly better than stalling.

Flexibility is another key ingredient of persistence. Despite our best efforts, we can't perfectly execute our plan, no matter how thoughtfully it was developed. Life is too complicated and chaotic. We have to deal with problems as minor as a leaky toilet and as major as a family member's chronic illness. If we don't adapt, we'll succumb to circumstance.

Still, we don't want to become women who have excuses for everything. You know the types—the ones who say they could accomplish so much if they just had more time, money, or support. They complain about being overwhelmed by personal problems, or say they're too focused on professional obligations. Many other women have faced more difficult circumstances than these, and yet have managed to succeed.

We also might be tempted to scale back our goals to make them achievable. Then we won't have to live with disappointment because we've made it impossible to fail. But we can't fool ourselves—we're not going to be fulfilled by the silhouette of a dream. ❧

Stay up and really burn the midnight oil. There are no compromises.

—LEONTYNE PRICE

I could not, at any age, be content to take my place by the fireside and simply look on. Life was meant to be lived. Curiosity must be kept alive. One must never, for whatever reason, turn his back on life.

—ELEANOR ROOSEVELT

Getting ahead in a difficult profession requires avid faith in yourself. You must be able to sustain yourself against staggering blows. There is no code of conduct to help beginners. That is why some people with mediocre talent, but with great inner drive, go much further than people with vastly superior talent.

—SOPHIA LOREN

Remember that the Devil doesn't sleep, but seeks our ruin in a thousand different ways.

—ANGELA MERICI

The wonderful thing about saints is that they were human. They lost their tempers, got hungry, scolded God, were egotistical or impatient in their turns, made mistakes and regretted them. Still they went on doggedly blundering toward heaven.

—Phyllis McGinley

A successful marriage requires falling in love many times, always with the same person.

—Mignon McLaughlin

Don't ask me to give in to this body of mine. I can't afford it. Between me and my body there must be a struggle until death.

—Saint Margaret of Cortona

Being human, we should bear all we can.

—Norma Meacock

Never think you've seen the last of anything.

—Eudora Welty

When you get into a tight place and everything goes against you, till it seems as though you could not hang on a minute longer, never give up then, for that is just the place and time that the tide will turn.

—Harriet Beecher Stowe

You may have to fight a battle more than once to win it.

—Margaret Thatcher

Our way is not soft grass, it's a mountain path with lots of rocks. But it goes upwards, forward, toward the sun.

—Dr. Ruth Westheimer

There are two parts to the creative endeavor: making something, then disseminating it.

—Jane Alexander

Live with no time out.

—Simone de Beauvoir

Only yield when you must, never "give up the ship," but fight on to the last "with a stiff upper lip!"

—Phoebe Cary

Never go to bed mad. Stay up and fight.

—Phyllis Diller

There is no point at which you can say, "Well, I'm successful now. I might as well take a nap."

—Carrie Fisher

I try. I am trying. I was trying. I will try. I shall in the meantime try. I sometimes have tried. I shall still by that time be trying.

—Diane Glancy

I can remember walking as a child. It was not customary to say you were fatigued. It was customary to complete the goal of the expedition.

—Katharine Hepburn

New links must be forged as old ones rust.

—JANE HOWARD

I am a stranger to half measures.

—MARITA GOLDEN

Hard times ain't quit and we ain't quit.

—MERIDEL LE SUEUR

Hope says to us constantly, "go on, go on," and leads us to the grave.

—FRANÇOISE D'AUBIGNÉ,
MARQUISE DE MAINTENON

When you put your hand to the plow, you can't put it down until you get to the end of the row.

—ALICE PAUL

The art of writing is the art of applying the seat of the pants to the seat of the chair.

—MARY HEATON VORSE

Chapter 27

LEARNING FROM MISTAKES

Throughout history, mistakes have led to discoveries.

There's the cook who made the first batch of potato chips by overcooking french fries, and the scientist who invented the pacemaker by putting the wrong wire in a recording device. Walt Disney filed for bankruptcy before launching his famous resort, and Oprah Winfrey was fired from her reporting job before she became one of the world's most famous personalities.

Our mistakes are important, too — they are often the foundation of personal growth. Although they're sometimes painful and embarrassing, our mistakes prove that we're living and learning.

Avoiding mistakes means we're avoiding choices that could change our lives. The thrill in living comes from trying new things, entering new

relationships, and plunging into opportunities—
any of which might not turn out the way we
envision. But any harm caused by such failures
is always less significant than the harm we do to
ourselves by living passively.

Sometimes it's difficult to forgive ourselves for
having made mistakes. We hold ourselves to
high standards, and we're discouraged when we
fall short of our own expectations. In fact, we
tend to judge ourselves more harshly than others do—people will accept an apology when
we admit our mistakes and genuinely try to correct them.

In return, we extend the same level of understanding to others. We've all gained experience
and wisdom—thanks to our mistakes. ❧

Life is not life unless you make mistakes.

—JOAN COLLINS

Mistakes are part of the dues one pays for a full life.

—SOPHIA LOREN

Flops are a part of life's menu and I've never been a girl to miss out on any of the courses.

—ROSALIND RUSSELL

Be aware that young people have to be able to make their own mistakes and that times change.

—GINA SHAPIRA

Mistakes are the usual bridge between inexperience and wisdom.

—PHYLLIS THEROUX

Sometimes what you want to do has to fail so you won't.

—MARGUERITTE HARMON BRO

An error gracefully acknowledged is a victory won.

—Caroline L. Gascoigne

There is no wisdom equal to that which comes after the event.

—Geraldine Jewsbury

I think success has no rules, but you can learn a great deal from failure.

—Jean Kerr

There are no mistakes, no coincidences. All events are blessings given to us to learn from.

—Elisabeth Kübler-Ross

We will be victorious if we have not forgotten how to learn.

—Rosa Luxemburg

It is very easy to forgive others their mistakes. It takes more grit and gumption to forgive them for having witnessed your own.

—JESSAMYN WEST

People fail forward to success.

—MARY KAY ASH

Apparent failure may hold in its rough shell the germs of a success that will blossom in time, and bear fruit throughout eternity.

—FRANCES ELLEN WATKINS HARPER

If you have made mistakes, even serious mistakes, there is always another chance for you.

—MARY PICKFORD

A new idea is rarely born like Venus attended by graces. More commonly it's modeled of baling wire and acne. More commonly it wheezes and tips over.

—MARGE PIERCY

A series of failures may culminate in the best possible result.

—Gisela Richter

No honest work of man or woman "fails"; it feeds the sum of all human action.

—Michelene Wandor

Some of the biggest failures I ever had were successes.

—Pearl S. Buck

There is a glory In a great mistake.

—Nathalia Crane

Show me a person who has never made a mistake and I'll show you somebody who has never achieved much.

—Joan Collins

Experience is how life catches up with us and teaches us to love and forgive each other.

—Judy Collins

Failure is just another way to learn how to do something right.

—MARIAN WRIGHT EDELMAN

It is not easy, but you have to be willing to make mistakes. And the earlier you make those mistakes, the better.

—JANE CAHILL PFEIFFER

Chapter 28

OVERCOMING WORRIES

Worrying can hijack our time and fill our days with negativity.

The list of concerns may start with trivial thoughts—the car repair might be expensive, we forgot our grocery list at home, rain could ruin the camping trip we've been planning. Gradually, our worries grow—what if those headaches are signs of a more serious medical problem? A few worries can explode into full-blown anxiety.

Worrying won't prevent things in life we can't control. If we can't prevent problems, perhaps we can focus our energy on fixing them. When we plan a camping trip, we're at the whim of the weather. We can make a backup plan—like turning the outdoor adventure into a hotel stay—or simply decide to make the best of the situation.

We might actually enjoy sleeping in nature with a gentle rain tapping against our tent.

Learning to cope with uncertainty in life helps us focus on important things and enjoy happy times. When we're able to stop the cycle of worrying, we can deal with problems more effectively. Once we develop solutions, we feel empowered. We've regained some of the control lost to anxiety.

We wouldn't want to be so carefree that we're careless. We don't want to be so successful at dismissing the small stuff that we start ignoring important things. A healthy dose of concern motivates us to solve problems and make good choices.

When we overcome our worries, we give ourselves energy for the things in life that matter—friends, family, and the time we share together. ❧

Of course I realized there was a measure of danger. Obviously I faced the possibility of not returning when I first considered going. Once faced and settled there really wasn't any good reason to refer to it again.

—AMELIA EARHART

Most people go through life dreading they'll have a traumatic experience.

—DIANE ARBUS

When fear seizes, change what you are doing. You are doing something wrong.

—JEAN CRAIGHEAD GEORGE

You will find a joy in overcoming obstacles.

—HELEN KELLER

Everybody knows if you are too careful you are so occupied in being careful that you are sure to stumble over something.

—GERTRUDE STEIN

Worries are the most stubborn habits in the world. Even after a poor man has won a huge lottery prize, he will still for months wake up in the night with a start, worrying about food and rent.

—VICKI BAUM

Although the world is full of suffering, it is also full of the overcoming of it.

—HELEN KELLER

Great self-destruction follows upon unfounded fear.

—URSULA K. LE GUIN

Worry is like racing the engine of an automobile without letting in the clutch.

—CORRIE TEN BOOM

Mountains appear more lofty the nearer they are approached, but great men resemble them not in this particular.

—LADY MARGUERITE BLESSINGTON

Worry a little bit every day and in a lifetime you will lose a couple of years. If something is wrong, fix it if you can. But train yourself not to worry. Worry never fixes anything.

—Mary Hemingway

Stop worrying about the potholes in the road and celebrate the journey!

—Barbara Hoffman

A man ninety years old was asked to what he attributed his longevity. "I reckon," he said, with a twinkle in his eye, "it's because most nights I went to bed and slept when I should have sat up and worried."

—Dorothea Kent

Worry is as useless as a handle on a snowball.

—Mitzi Chandler

Fear is created not by the world around us, but in the mind, by what we think is going to happen.

—Elizabeth Gawain

You just have to learn not to care about the dust mites under the beds.

—Margaret Mead

It is far harder to kill a phantom than a reality.

—Virginia Woolf

Worry less about what other people think about you, and more about what you think about them.

—Fay Weldon

You can't start worrying about what's going to happen. You get spastic enough worrying about what's happening now.

—Lauren Bacall

The really frightening thing about middle age is that you know you'll grow out of it!

—DORIS DAY

A request not to worry…is perhaps the least soothing message capable of human utterance.

—MIGNON G. EBERHART

We have to fight them daily, like fleas, those many small worries about the morrow, for they sap our energies.

—ETTY HILLESUM

T'ain't worthwhile to wear a day all out before it comes.

—SARAH ORNE JEWETT

A worried man could borrow a lot of trouble with practically no collateral.

—HELEN NIELSEN

Chapter 29

ACCEPTING UNCERTAINTY

Living is an adventure into the great unknown. No matter how much we study the science of life, no matter how much we ponder our purpose on earth, we have no hint of what the future will bring.

It's thrilling—and a little terrifying.

When we're feeling anxious about the future, everything seems fragile and uncertain—the relationships we've nurtured, the possessions we've accumulated, the image we've constructed of ourselves. We don't know whether our life's journey will end in hours or decades. We don't know whether the years ahead will be filled with trials or good fortune. And we're careful about using our history as a guide for the future. Clinging to the past hinders our ability to change our lives and achieve our goals.

What we do know is that life unfolds in a series of stages, each with its own pleasures and challenges. The adventure lies in the discovery of each stage: learning about the world as children, defining ourselves as young adults and, as grown women, building a life and sharing it with others.

The uncertainty can be unsettling, but its mystery opens our eyes to life's miracles—the changing seasons, the wonders of nature, the enchantment of childbirth. Scientists have come a long way in explaining the *how*, but the human race continues to ponder the *why*.

The key to reducing stress is learning to accept uncertainty about the future. Instead of allowing anxiety to overwhelm us, we can try to marvel at today's wonders while looking forward to tomorrow's adventures. ❧

Experience has no textbooks nor proxies. She demands that her pupils answer to her roll-call personally.

—Minna Antrim

All decisions are made on insufficient evidence.

—Rita Mae Brown

It's quite possible to leave your home for a walk in the early morning air and return a different person— beguiled, enchanted.

—Mary Chase

Life is not orderly. No matter how we try to make life so, right in the middle of it we die, lose a leg, fall in love, drop a jar of applesauce.

—Natalie Goldberg

Time has told me less than I need to know.

—Gwen Harwood

Truly nothing is to be expected but the unexpected.

—ALICE JAMES

The only thing that makes life possible is permanent, intolerable uncertainty, not knowing what comes next.

—URSULA K. LE GUIN

Nothing, perhaps, is strange, once you have accepted life itself, the great strange business which includes all lesser strangeness.

—ROSE MACAULAY

None of us knows what the next change is going to be, what unexpected opportunity is just around the corner, waiting a few months or a few years to change all the tenor of our lives.

—KATHLEEN NORRIS

The shortest period of time lies between the minute you put some money away for a rainy day and the unexpected arrival of rain.

—JANE BRYANT QUINN

I wanted a perfect ending. Now I've learned, the hard way, that some poems don't rhyme, and some stories don't have a clear beginning, middle, and end. Life is about not knowing, having to change, taking the moment and making the best of it without knowing what's going to happen next.

—GILDA RADNER

Where will I be five years from now? I delight in not knowing.

—MARLO THOMAS

We live in an epoch in which the solid ground of our preconceived ideas shakes daily under our certain feet.

—BARBARA WARD

I said here's the river I want to flow on, here's the direction I want to go, and put my boat in. I was ready for the river to take unexpected turns and present obstacles.

—Nancy Woodhull

There is no security, no assurance that because we wrote something good two months ago, we will do it again. Actually, every time we begin, we wonder how we ever did it before.

—Natalie Goldberg

No one from the beginning of time has had security.

—Eleanor Roosevelt

Life is uncertain. Eat dessert first.

—Ernestine Ulmer

No great deed is done by falterers who ask for certainty.

—George Eliot (Mary Ann Evans)

The world is quite right. It does not have to be consistent.

—CHARLOTTE P. GILMAN

Isn't it splendid to think of all the things there are to find out about? It just makes me feel glad to be alive—it's such an interesting world. It wouldn't be half so interesting if we knew all about everything, would it? There'd be no scope for imagination then, would there?

—L. M. MONTGOMERY

It's astonishing in this world how things don't turn out at all the way you expect them to.

—AGATHA CHRISTIE

Chapter 30

SHOWING COURAGE

Fear has an important purpose—it protects us from physical harm. But misplaced apprehension can paralyze us and take all the joy out of living.

It takes courage to build a rich and joyful life. It's not the same kind of courage that leads us to confront a burglar. Rather, it's an inner strength that helps us take risks, pursue our dreams, and stand up for our convictions.

When we give our energy to fear, it becomes a powerful, controlling force. The negative energy can infect every aspect of our lives. Apprehension about rejection and failure stops us from trying new things. We lose the chance to develop more meaningful relationships.

Identifying our fear is the first step in building a reservoir of courage. If the idea of giving a public presentation is nerve-racking, we should ask ourselves, is our fear really about speaking in front of a group—or are we afraid our ideas might be rejected? If we're hesitant to take a new job, is it because the position doesn't seem right for us—or are we simply afraid of change?

Courage comes more easily with practice. Once we've faced one fear, we have the confidence and experience to face another. But sometimes the outcome is distressing. Confronting a boss about unethical behavior could get us fired. In that case, the price of courage is our job. The price of fear, however, is worse—it's being forced to live with the shame of doing nothing. ❧

Courage is very important. Like a muscle, it is strengthened by use.

—RUTH GORDON

I think laughter may be a form of courage....As humans we sometimes stand tall and look into the sun and laugh, and I think we are never more brave than when we do that.

—LINDA ELLERBEE

I became more courageous by doing the very things I needed to be courageous for—first, a little, and badly. Then, bit by bit, more and better. Being avidly—sometimes annoyingly—curious and persistent about discovering how others were doing what I wanted to do.

—AUDRE LORDE

I have accepted fear as a part of my life—specifically the fear of change....I have gone ahead despite the pounding in the heart that says: turn back.

—ERICA JONG

I realized that if what we call human nature can be changed, then absolutely anything is possible. And from that moment, my life changed.

—SHIRLEY MACLAINE

I believe that anyone can conquer fear by doing the things he fears to do, provided he keeps doing them until he gets a record of successful experiences behind him.

—ELEANOR ROOSEVELT

A woman's life can really be a succession of lives, each revolving around some emotionally compelling situation or challenge, and each marked off by some intense experience.

—WALLIS, DUCHESS OF WINDSOR

Any coward can fight a battle when he's sure of winning; but give me the man who has pluck to fight when he's sure of losing. That's my way, sir; and there are many victories worse than defeat.

—GEORGE ELIOT (MARY ANN EVANS)

There were always in me, two women at least, one woman desperate and bewildered, who felt she was drowning and another who would leap into a scene, as upon a stage, conceal her true emotions because they were weaknesses, helplessness, despair, and present to the world only a smile, an eagerness, curiosity, enthusiasm, interest.

—ANAÏS NIN

Grab the broom of anger and drive off the beast of fear.

—ZORA NEALE HURSTON

Become so wrapped up in something that you forget to be afraid.

—LADY BIRD JOHNSON

To keep our faces toward change, and behave like free spirits in the presence of fate, is strength undefeatable.

—HELEN KELLER

Being "brave" means doing or facing something frightening.... Being "fearless" means being without fear.

—PENELOPE LEACH

I am deliberate and afraid of nothing.

—AUDRE LORDE

There are some women who seem to be born without fear, just as there are people who are born without the ability to feel pain.... Providence appears to protect such women, maybe out of astonishment.

—MARGARET ATWOOD

Fear is a sign—usually a sign that I'm doing something right.

—ERICA JONG

Courage is fear that has said its prayers.

—DOROTHY BERNARD

If you are brave too often, people will come to expect it of you.

—Mignon McLaughlin

It is not in the still calm of life, or the repose of a pacific station, that great characters are formed…great necessities call out great virtues.

—Abigail Adams

What I emphasize is for people to make choices based not on fear, but on what really gives them a sense of fulfillment.

—Pauline Rose Chance

Life shrinks or expands in proportion to one's courage.

—Anaïs Nin

In order to feel anything, you need strength.

—Anna Maria Ortese

Chapter 31

ADJUSTING TO CHANGE

We know that change is exciting and fulfilling—not to mention inevitable. Then why is it so hard?

Our daydreams revolve around change. We melt into thoughts of moving to a different city, launching a new career, and meeting exciting people. The emphasis is on different, new, and exciting. But in real life, change is rarely smooth. In fact, it's typically a source of stress.

How can we possibly feel stress after taking a new job when the pay is better, the work is interesting, and the co-workers are wonderful? Because it's different. We have to function on high alert. Not only are there new people to meet and new skills to learn, it's an entirely different culture with nuances that require study and practice. It's an exhausting process.

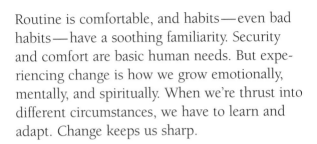

Routine is comfortable, and habits—even bad habits—have a soothing familiarity. Security and comfort are basic human needs. But experiencing change is how we grow emotionally, mentally, and spiritually. When we're thrust into different circumstances, we have to learn and adapt. Change keeps us sharp.

While some of us cling to routines and tradition, others are change "junkies." We've had phases in our lives where change didn't have to be imposed on us; we sought it out. But change for the sake of change only means *different*—it doesn't necessarily mean *better*.

Regardless of what brings it on, change is introducing us to a stage in life that we will either love or dread. Focusing on the excitement, instead of our fear, will help us through the adjustment. And when we're finally comfortable with our new circumstances, we can look back and see our growth. ❧

Life is change. Growth is optional. Choose wisely.

— KAREN KAISER CLARK

The challenges of change are always hard. It is important that we begin to unpack those challenges that confront this nation and realize that we each have a role that requires us to change and become more responsible for shaping our own future.

— HILLARY RODHAM CLINTON

They were so strong in their beliefs that there came a time when it hardly mattered what exactly those beliefs were; they all fused into a single stubbornness.

— LOUISE ERDRICH

All change is not growth, as all movement is not forward.

— ELLEN GLASGOW

It's the most unhappy people who most fear change.

— MIGNON MCLAUGHLIN

The mind of the most logical thinker goes so easily from one point to another that it is not hard to mistake motion for progress.

—Margaret Collier Graham

Our fathers valued change for the sake of its results; we value it in the act.

—Alice Meynell

Life is measured by the rapidity of change, the succession of influences that modify the being.

—George Eliot (Mary Ann Evans)

You don't have to be afraid of change. You don't have to worry about what's being taken away. Just look to see what's been added.

—Jackie Greer

Change is the constant, the signal for rebirth, the egg of the phoenix.

—Christina Baldwin

Everyday life confronts us with new problems to be solved which force us to adjust our old programs accordingly.

—Dr. Ann Faraday

No one can persuade another to change. Each of us guards a gate of change that can only be opened from the inside. We cannot open the gate of another, either by argument or emotional appeal.

—Marilyn Ferguson

Changes are not only possible and predictable, but to deny them is to be an accomplice to one's own unnecessary vegetation.

—Gail Sheehy

We measure success and depth by length and time, but it is possible to have a deep relationship that doesn't always stay the same.

—Barbara Hershey

I have found that sitting in a place where you have never sat before can be inspiring.

—DODIE SMITH

We're just getting started. We're just beginning to meet what will be the future—we've got the Model T.

—GRACE MURRAY HOPPER

Continuity gives us roots; change gives us branches, letting us stretch and grow and reach new heights.

—PAULINE R. KEZER

Nothing should be permanent except struggle with the dark side within ourselves.

—SHIRLEY MACLAINE

Things good in themselves…perfectly valid in the integrity of their origins, become fetters if they cannot alter.

—FREYA STARK

I've learned that you'll never be disappointed if you always keep an eye on uncharted territory, where you'll be challenged and growing and having fun.

—KIRSTIE ALLEY

One of the dreariest spots on life's road is the point of conviction that nothing will ever again happen to you.

—FAITH BALDWIN

Those interested in perpetuating present conditions are always in tears about the marvelous past that is about to disappear, without having so much as a smile for the young future.

—SIMONE DE BEAUVOIR

The most amazing thing about little children…was their fantastic adaptability.

—KRISTIN HUNTER

People change and forget to tell each other.

—LILLIAN HELLMAN

Chapter 32

GROWING FROM ADVERSITY

It seems every day we see people on the news who've suffered a terrible loss. They've lost homes to disasters, their loved ones to accidents, or their sense of security to criminal acts.

What the news media often don't show are the kindhearted members of the community who invariably come forward in these crises and open their hearts, homes, and wallets.

During difficult times, we can find small comfort in knowing that adversity teaches us the skills to cope. Problems are an inevitable part of life. Having tools to solve problems helps us survive the hard times and move on to better days.

It's not so much problems that make us stronger and better people; it's the process of working through them. At first, we feel stunned and overwhelmed. We wonder how we'll get through it. Then we realize we have no choice but to push through the crisis—one problem at a time, one day at a time.

As life returns to normal, and the problems are resolved, we can look back and marvel at our strength. We didn't cope with everything perfectly, but we did the best we could under enormous stress.

We emerge from adversity stronger, wiser, and more capable. We have a new awareness of our blessings—not just our possessions, but the people who care enough to support and love us. The gift of adversity is perspective. ◐

If you haven't had at least a slight poetic crack in the heart, you have been cheated by nature.

—PHYLLIS BATTELLE

When something bad happens to me, I think I'm able to deal with it in a pretty good way. That makes me lucky. Some people fall apart at the first little thing that happens.

—CHRISTIE BRINKLEY

True knowledge comes only through suffering.

—ELIZABETH BARRETT BROWNING

Suffering raises up those souls that are truly great; it is only small souls that are made mean-spirited by it.

—ALEXANDRA DAVID-NÉEL

He disposes Doom who hath suffered him.

—EMILY DICKINSON

Prosperity provideth, but adversity proveth friends.

—Queen Elizabeth I

Suffering has always been with us, does it really matter in what form it comes? All that matters is how we bear it and how we fit it into our lives.

—Etty Hillesum

At every step the child should be allowed to meet the real experience of life; the thorns should never be plucked from his roses.

—Ellen Key

You can't be brave if you've only had wonderful things happen to you.

—Mary Tyler Moore

Troubles cured you salty as a country ham, smoky to the taste, thick-skinned and tender inside.

—Marge Piercy

In all things preserve integrity; and the consciousness of thine own uprightness will alleviate the toil of business, soften the hardness of ill-success and disappointments, and give thee an humble confidence before God, when the ingratitude of man, or the iniquity of the times may rob thee of other rewards.

—Barbara Paley

Difficulties, opposition, criticism—these things are meant to be overcome, and there is a special joy in facing them and in coming out on top. It is only when there is nothing but praise that life loses its charm and I begin to wonder what I should do about it.

—Vijaya Lakshmi Pandit

Women are like tea bags; put them in hot water and they get stronger.

—Eleanor Roosevelt

Hot water is my native element. I was in it as a baby, and I have never seemed to get out of it ever since.

—Dame Edith Sitwell

However confused the scene of our life appears, however torn we may be who now do face that scene, it can be faced, and we can go on to be whole.

—Muriel Rukeyser

If you have to be careful because of oppression and censorship, this pressure produces diamonds.

—Tatyana Tolstaya

We say: mad with joy. We should say: wise with grief.

—Marguerite Yourcenar

It is only after an unknown number of unrecorded labors, after a host of noble hearts have succumbed in discouragement, convinced that their cause is lost; it is only then that cause triumphs.

—Madame Guizot

To be tested is good. The challenged life may be the best therapist.

—Gail Sheehy

It constantly happens that the Lord permits a soul to fall so that it may grow humbler.

—TERESA OF ÁVILA

Without the burden of afflictions it is impossible to reach the height of grace. The gift of grace increases as the struggles increase.

—SAINT ROSE OF LIMA

I have learned in the great University of Hard Knocks a philosophy that no woman who has had an easy life ever acquires. I have learned to live each day as it comes, and not to borrow trouble by dreading tomorrow. It is the dark menace of the future that makes cowards of us.

—DOROTHY DIX

There is often in people to whom "the worst" has happened an almost transcendent freedom, for they have faced "the worst" and survived it.

—CAROL PEARSON